SOURCES OF CIVILIZATION IN THE WEST

Crane Brinton and Robert Lee Wolff,
General Editors

ROBIN W. WINKS, the editor of this volume in
the Sources of Civilization in the West series, is
Professor of History at Yale University. He has
written numerous books and articles, which include
*Canada and the U...
Years, British Imp...
Literature in Can...
phy of the British
tory of Malaysia (...
West Indian Unio...
in England, Austra........ ..., Malaysia, and Leb-
anon.

THE AGE

OF IMPERIALISM

Edited by

Robin W. Winks

PRENTICE-HALL, INC.
Englewood Cliffs, New Jersey

A SPECTRUM BOOK

Current printing (last number):

10 9 8 7 6 5 4 3 2 1

PRENTICE-HALL INTERNATIONAL, INC. (*London*)
PRENTICE-HALL OF AUSTRALIA, PTY. LTD. (*Sydney*)
PRENTICE-HALL OF CANADA, LTD. (*Toronto*)
PRENTICE-HALL OF INDIA PRIVATE LIMITED (*New Delhi*)
PRENTICE-HALL OF JAPAN, INC. (*Tokyo*)

FOREWORD

Though the European acquisition of some four-fifths of the earth's surface may not all have been accomplished in a fit of absence of mind, it is surely true that the educated western public until very recently has treated this key phenomenon of recent human history with a general lack of attention. Only in the years since the end of World War II—with the achievement of political freedom by the Philippines, India, Pakistan, Indonesia, and British, French, and Belgian Africa, and with the warfare in the Congo, in Malaya, in Algeria, and in Vietnam—have non-specialists been forced by the very pressure of events to begin to realize the enormous importance of imperialism. What has it meant to the conqueror and settler, what to the inhabitants of the conquered and settled regions?

To these enormous questions Professor Winks addresses himself in this collection of vivid excerpts from the writings of the practitioners, the theorists, and the victims (or beneficiaries?) of imperialism themselves. Here you will find Marco Polo and Camoens from the early periods of exploration, and the first reports by Europeans on the aborigines of the South Pacific and Australasia; expressions by the imperialists in person of all the chief motives for settlement, exploitation, and new government; the theoretical conclusions of Hobson, Lenin, Schumpeter, and Frantz Fanon. How was it done? Here are sample treaties, illustrating the various stages and forms of European involvement, extortion, protection, from early days down to mandates and trusteeships, and the various degrees of persuasion, bribery, and force. Here too is the western conscience at work, making the best—and often a good best too—of its moral qualms by paternalism, education, social betterment, and even courtesy toward the natives. Here is Joyce Cary, the novelist, reminiscing about his days as a District Officer in Nigeria, and here is K. M. Panikkar giving an Indian view of European nations in Asia.

I have found this book absorbingly interesting to read: each of the selections gives a new dimension to the subject. And if there are more passages dealing with the British experience than with that of other imperial nations, and more on Southeast Asia and on Australia than one might have expected, this for me gives focus to a collection that might otherwise have seemed diffuse. I think this book will tempt the beginner to continue his reading, and predict that it will hold the attention of many an old hand at the subject who may never before have encountered this passage or that, and who finds his views altering as he considers their implications.

Robert Lee Wolff
Coolidge Professor of History
Harvard University

CONTENTS

IV. EVALUATION

Introduction

Western man has just begun to realize what the rest of the world has known for a long time: that one of the most sweeping, and fundamental, periods of change in the world's history was that which we label the Age of Imperialism. Together with the Reformation, the long period of exploration and discovery, the Industrial Revolution, and post-Einsteinian physics, imperialism has brought upheaval and change to major portions of the globe. While the impact of European customs, administrative systems, and moral injunctions may have been less sweeping than the imperialists themselves thought, the impress of European technology, trading patterns, and languages was nothing less than revolutionary, in the proper and old-fashioned meaning of that abused word.

Consider the dimensions of imperialism. In 1930, when European administration in the non-European world was already on the wane, 84 per cent of the land surface of the globe was under the control of Western, white nations. The very terminology of the world, of geography itself, was Eurocentric: Near East, Middle East, Far East. Far, and eastern, from what, one might ask; to an Australian, and indeed to an American, Japan and China were not always far and certainly not to the east (a fact Australians recognized after World War II by substituting Near North for the European-imposed designation). Entire peoples who had no collective name for themselves were given, or took, such names in the face of European encroachments: the Navajo, the Maori, and many cultures ranging across Africa. Normative standards for progress were based upon European concepts of economic growth, political stability, desirable social customs, and national status. Between 1947 and 1963 a single imperial power, Great Britain, saw 750 million former subjects become citizens of newly independent states. By a substantial margin, the majority of those who stand to speak in the United Nations Assembly today represent countries which, but 25 years ago, were the colonies of Britain, France, The Netherlands, Belgium, or the United States.

The imperial experience was far-reaching in time as well as in space. Through their use of superior sailing vessels, the maritime nations of Portugal, Spain, Holland, and later France and Britain were able to make all of the shores of the seas their neighbors. While Chinese junks journeyed from Canton south around the Malay archipelago to the Malabar Coast and while Arab *dhows* reached out across the Indian Ocean and down the length of East Africa, such ventures

1

seldom led to permanent settlements. Where conquest did follow, the environment was not always remade in the image of the conquerer, for Islam was willing to let other faiths coexist under the sword, and Hinduism placed far greater emphasis on the next life than on this. Europeans, however, armed with an aggressive Christianity, whether Protestant or Roman Catholic, chose not only to exchange goods and ideas but to rule, to change, and to convert as well. A conviction of moral superiority, a genuine curiosity about the world that lay across the horizon, and clear technological dominance created, extended, and preserved the long period of European hegemony. Thus from the fifteenth century until the middle of the twentieth, the processes of colonization, imperialism, and decolonization would form an important link between East and West, black and white, the have and the have-not peoples.

In the final analysis imperialism—the process by which one people gained and maintained power over another, usually of a different race —was more a cluster of attitudes than an economic or political policy. The recipient of the good and ill that imperialism brought, whether Bantu, Apache, Maori, or Malay, became one of the wretched of the earth, a man who knew that life's fundamental decisions were being made for him somewhere else, by people who might or might not understand his needs, frustrations, and desires, by a government alien, self-imposed, and predominantly white. Thus racism, itself a state of mind, became inextricably mixed with the imperial experience, until Britishers forgot that the epithet "wog," which originally designated a Westernized Oriental Gentleman, was a dirty word, one of the many in the vocabulary of imperialism.

That vocabulary was an expanding one, able to accommodate terms of racial opprobrium and of patronizing endearment, able to encompass the outright appropriation of native lands to Crown, federal government, or company while speaking of the protection of native rights. Imperialists were a paradoxical people, for that which they practiced was a paradox: bringing immense benefits to millions, equally immense burdens to yet other millions; the experience of imperialism to him who controlled and to him who was controlled was a mixed one. One cannot speak, now and possibly never (although some historians do so) of a "balance sheet of imperialism," for this is to imply that Western standards may continue to be the normative ones by which judgment is passed upon an experience of 500 years, as though one might award a point system to the colonial power which built good roads, provided for education, sanitation, and peaceful frontiers, and also massacred innocent women and children within the locked gates of Amritsar. It is patently unfair for the heirs of the imperialists to judge now the fruits of their fathers; it is equally unfair for the "victims" to report their sole patrimony as victimization. Not until the imperial revolution has played out its last century, still with us, can one suggest—and then upon standards other than those we can now use—what the fundamental influence of the imperialist has been.

This collection, then, presents a selection of statements by means of which the reader may grope toward his own interim conclusion, a succession of documents through which he may see what imperialism was, at certain times and certain places. Whether imperialism paid or not—a favorite question of historians, and a not unimportant one—remains less important than the question of how the symbols, the rhetoric, the thought processes of the imperial revolution became the heritage of all of us, black, white, European, African, who would attempt to understand the intricacies of our human experience. As he lay dying, King George V asked, "How is the Empire?" We, too, must ask this historical question, even though our answer may well be quite unlike that of the Prime Minister who replied to his King, "All's well, sir, with the Empire."

A Note on the Documents

The documents that follow were selected with three views in mind: that they be representative of a particular problem, that they be interesting in themselves, and that, read consecutively, they might possibly lead to a greater understanding of imperialism and its effects. In short, the reader should put to himself the customary questions of the historian who interrogates a primary source: is it true, is it interesting, is it important? Emphasis has been placed on the British empire, in that Britain embraced the best, as well as some of the worst, of imperialism, and achieved the greatest imperial sway, but other imperial powers have not been neglected. "Source" was taken to include judgments passed by those who speak now on past events, provided these speakers were former colonial officials or eyewitnesses; no purely secondary work has been drawn upon, in keeping with the other volumes in this series. The editor has removed the footnotes that appeared in the original sources; with this exception, all omissions are indicated by ellipses. All figures are identified, if not by the authors themselves, then by the editor in footnotes or brackets on the first occasion of their presence in the text, but not thereafter, on the assumption that the collection is to be read as a whole. All of the footnotes were supplied by the editor. The spelling and punctuation of the original documents was retained, although modern forms for proper names were used in the headnotes.

Part One

RECONNAISSANCE

The great age of exploration and discovery was a product of the Renaissance, when men were seeking out a new order of things, new commodities, new lives, and new lands. In 1516, when Thomas More's description of an island state, *Utopia,* was published, Duarte Barbosa, a Portuguese administrator in Goa, on the south Indian shore, was just leaving his post. More's Raphael Hythlodaeus, while fictitious, was real enough in his possession of the darting sense of curiosity that marked the age; he was "more anxious for travel than about the grave" and certain that Europe could learn much from other races not yet even seen. Barbosa shared this conviction, learned the Malayalam language of the south Indians among whom he lived, and wrote a book which described in detail the dwellings, commerce, government, and produce of the places he visited. Travellers' tales, whether fictitious but sound, purely descriptive but comprehensive, or—as with the wild fantasies of Sir John Mandeville—false and misleading, were to help shape the Europeans' attitudes toward travel, discovery, and foreign lands.

Perhaps most importantly, such accounts shaped the nature of cultural contacts for decades to come. That there were black men in Africa and brown in India was strange enough, and that they followed unknown gods, muttered in incomprehensible languages, and often went naked was stranger yet. But upon closer examination they proved to be human enough, and even mundane enough, to force those who wished to report of the dangers of their adventures—which were very real in any case—or who wished to tell a good tale, to accentuate the odd and forget the explicable. Were strange men wanted? Then strange men with strange customs would be found, or, if not found, invented. Did black men have souls? Probably not, for they appeared to feel no pain, did not cry when parted from their children, and those windows upon the soul, the eyes, reflected back but

4

their blackness. One crewman aboard an exploring craft systematically shot a number of natives to learn whether they might bleed. Martin Frobisher's men undressed an Eskimo to discover whether she (for such the figure was revealed to be) was a witch, and they were none the wiser for their experiment. If the people one encountered were not truly strange, then those just across the horizon, at the next landfall, would be dressed in solid gold, would have eyes in the middle of their foreheads, would be ruled by giant women, or would be able to wrap themselves with their ears serving as blankets. Under the impact of such expectations, coupled with the Renaissance desire to catalogue, to measure, and to classify all that was seen, grew assumptions —already well nurtured by other sources of racial thought—about the differences in men, the gulfs that separated them, the urgent need for the spread of Christianity, and the inferiority of one group as opposed to another.

Imperialism began before exploration, in the minds of men. It was related to a natural, even noble, desire to see all things, to know all things, to taste and hold all things. When Ludovico di Varthema sailed from Venice in 1502 to cross the Levant, to round Cape Comorin, to visit the great Hindu kingdom of Vijayanagar, to describe Malacca on the west coast of the Malayan Archipelago, he was compelled, he wrote (and while a portion of his itinerary is open to question, there is little reason to doubt his motives), out of a desire to see for himself the wonders of a wondrous world:

> There have been many men who have devoted themselves to the investigation of the things of this world and by the aid of divers studies, journeys, and very exact relations have endeavored to accomplish their desire. Others again of more perspicacious understandings, to whom the earth has not sufficed, such as the Chaldeans and Phoenicians, have begun to traverse the highest regions of Heaven with careful observations and watchings: from all which I know that each has gained most deserved and high praise from others and abundant satisfaction to themselves. Wherefore, I, feeling a very great desire for similar results, and leaving alone the Heavens as a burthen more suitable for the shoulders of Atlas and Hercules, determined to investigate some small portion of this our terrestrial globe; and not having any inclination . . . to arrive at my desire by study or conjectures, I determined, personally, and with my own eyes, to endeavor to ascertain the situations of places, the qualities of peoples, the diversities of animals, the varieties of the fruit-bearing and odoriferous trees . . . [of the East] remembering well that the testimony of one eye-witness is worth more than ten hear-says.

Here, with words that Shakespeare would employ, was a forerunner of *The Tempest,* that great Elizabethan document that combined all those elements of the strange, the utopian, the far-flung and foreign.

These elements in turn produced the state of mind which impelled Europeans to seek and explore new lands. By 1589, when Richard Hakluyt had brought together in his work, *The Principall Navigations, Voiages and Discoveries of the English Nation made by Sea or over Land* . . . , the many texts that would comprise the second Bible of the explorer, this impulse to see for oneself had also become an impulse to see, and to acquire, for one's nation. Columbus had long before discovered his America, Balboa had looked upon the broad Pacific, Pigafetta had recorded (although not published) the exploits of Magellan during his voyage around the world, Africa had been penetrated, and the first frustrating probings for northwest and northeast passages had been abandoned.

The documents that follow reveal something of the attitudes of the explorers, of the men responsible for many of the initial contacts between the non-Western world and Europe. Even in the centuries that followed, as interior exploration replaced the searching of the seas, the sense of wonder—and of arrogance—continued to insure that, in the moment of first contact, it would almost always be the European, the man who had journeyed and had the knowledge of other lands at his fingertips, who had technological superiority, fire-power, and the decks of gunboats from which to speak, who initiated that contact. If all that they saw was, as Richard Chancellor wrote of Moscovie, "very rare and wonderfull," it was also decaying: the natural life, the landscape, and resources of the lands were richly praised, while the people were seen to represent civilizations which, while once of a high order, were on a long downward slide into oblivion. As Warren Hastings, Britain's administrator in Bengal, wrote in 1777 in another context, "All that the wisest institutions" could do, in a temporary possession, was "to protract that decay, which sooner or later must end it."

Marco Polo in the East

The best, and most widely known, medieval account of travel in Asia was written by Marco Polo. Son of a Venetian merchant, Nicolo, who earlier had visited Peking, Marco resided in that city, where he was a trusted emissary for Kublai Khan, and from which he travelled throughout the East from 1272 or 1273 until 1292. His much-copied record of what he saw was based on firsthand observation, a sceptical unwillingness to incorporate fantastic tales which he had not verified for himself, and close scrutiny of the people around him. The following extract is representative, drawing upon his report of what he saw in India and Zipangu (Japan). Here geography is circumscribed, and emphasis is placed upon data, description, and measurement. In keeping with the explorers who would follow, Marco could explain what he had seen only in comparative terms, by relating that which he saw to that which was done "in the same manner as we," by false analogies rather than by permitting the unique elements of the cultures he encountered to retain their uniqueness.

From *The Travels of Marco Polo* (New York: Orion Press, n.d.), pp. 259–66.

[W]e shall now . . . proceed to . . . India, the admirable circumstances of which shall be related. We shall commence with a description of the ships employed by the merchants, which are built of fir-timber. They have a single deck, and below this the space is divided into about sixty small cabins, fewer or more, according to the size of the vessels, each of them affording accommodation for one merchant. They are provided with a good helm. They have four masts, with as many sails, and some of them have two masts which can be set up and lowered again, as may be found necessary. Some ships of the larger class have, besides to the number of thirteen bulk-heads or divisions in the hold, formed of thick planks let into each other. The object of these is to guard against accidents which may occasion the vessels to spring a leak, such as striking on a rock or receiving a stroke from a whale, a circumstance that not unfrequently occurs; for, when sailing at night, the motion through the waves causes a white foam that attracts the notice of the hungry animal. In expectation of meeting with food, it rushes violently to the spot, strikes the ship, and often forces in some part of the bottom. The water, running in at the place where the injury has been sustained, makes its way to the well, which is always kept clear. The crew, upon discovering the situation of the leak, immediately remove the goods from the division affected by the water, which, in consequence of the boards being so

7

well fitted, cannot pass from one division to another. They then repair the damage, and return the goods to that place in the hold from whence they had been taken. The ships are all doubleplanked; that is, they have a course of sheathing-boards laid over the planking in every part. These are caulked with oakum both withinside and without, and are fastened with iron nails. They are not coated with pitch, as the country does not produce that article, but the bottoms are smeared over with the following preparation. The people take quick-lime and hemp, which latter they cut small, and with these, when pounded together, they mix oil procured from a certain tree, making of the whole a kind of unguent, which retains its viscous properties more firmly, and is a better material than pitch.

Ships of the largest size require a crew of three hundred men; others, two hundred; and some, one hundred and fifty only, according to their greater or less bulk. They carry from five to six thousand baskets of pepper. In former times they were of greater burthen than they are at present; but the violence of the sea having in many places broken up the islands, and especially in some of the principal ports, there is a want of depth of water for vessels of such draught, and they have on that account been built, in latter times, of a smaller size. The vessels are likewise moved with oars or sweeps, each of which requires four men to work it. Those of the larger class are accompanied by two or three large barks, capable of containing about one thousand baskets of pepper, and are manned with sixty, eighty, or one hundred sailors. These small craft are often employed to tow the larger, when working their oars, or even under sail, provided the wind be on the quarter, but not when right aft, because, in that case, the sails of the larger vessel must becalm those of the smaller, which would, in consequence, be run down. The ships also carry with them as many as ten small boats, for the purpose of carrying out anchors, for fishing, and a variety of other services. They are slung over the sides, and lowered into the water when there is occasion to use them. The barks are in like manner provided with their small boats. When a ship, having been on a voyage for a year or more, stands in need of repair, the practice is to give her a course of sheathing over the original boarding, forming a third course, which is caulked and paid in the same manner as the others; and this, when she needs further repairs, is repeated, even to the number of six layers, after which she is condemned as unserviceable and not seaworthy. Having thus described the shipping, we shall proceed to the account of India; but in the first instance we shall speak of certain islands in the part of the ocean where we are at present, and shall commence with the island named Zipangu.

Zipangu is an island in the eastern ocean, situated at the distance of about fifteen hundred miles from the mainland, or coast of Manji. It is of considerable size; its inhabitants have fair complexions, are well made, and are civilized in their manners. Their religion is the worship of idols. They are independent of every foreign power, and governed only by their own kings. They have gold in the greatest abundance, its sources being inexhaustible, but as the king does not allow of its being exported, few merchants visit the country, nor is it frequented by much shipping from other parts. To this circumstance we are to attribute the extraordinary richness of the sovereign's palace, according to what we are told by those who have access to the place. The entire roof is covered with a plating of gold, in the same manner as we cover houses, or more properly churches, with lead. The ceilings of the halls are of the same precious metal; many of the apartments have small tables of pure gold, of considerable thickness; and the windows also have golden ornaments. So vast, indeed, are the riches of the palace, that it is impossible to convey an idea of them. In this island there are pearls also, in large quantities, of a red (pink) colour, round in shape, and of great size, equal in value to, or even exceeding that of the white pearls. It is customary with one part of the inhabitants to bury their dead, and with another part to burn them. The former have a practice of putting one of these pearls into the mouth of the corpse. There are also found there a number of precious stones.

Of so great celebrity was the wealth of this island, that a desire was excited in the breast of the grand khan Kublaï, now reigning, to make the conquest of it, and to annex it to his dominions. In order to effect this, he fitted out a numerous fleet, and embarked a large body of troops, under the command of two of his principal officers . . . The expedition sailed from the ports of Zai-tun and Kin-sai, and, crossing the intermediate sea, reached the island in safety; but in consequence of a jealousy that arose between the two commanders, one of whom treated the plans of the other with contempt and resisted the execution of his orders, they were unable to gain possession of any city or fortified place, with the exception of one only, which was carried by assault, the garrison having refused to surrender. Directions were given for putting the whole to the sword, and in obedience thereto the heads of all were cut off, excepting of eight persons, who, by the efficacy of a diabolical charm, consisting of a jewel or amulet introduced into the right arm, between the skin and the flesh, were rendered secure from the effects of iron, either to kill or wound. Upon this discovery being made, they were beaten with a heavy wooden club, and presently died.

It happened, after some time, that a north wind began to blow with great force, and the ships of the Tartars, which lay near the shore of the island, were driven foul of each other. It was determined thereupon, in a council of the officers on board, that they ought to disengage themselves from the land; and accordingly, as soon as the troops were re-embarked, they stood out to sea. The gale, however, increased to so violent a degree that a number of the vessels foundered. The people belonging to them, by floating upon pieces of the wreck, saved themselves upon an island lying about four miles from the coast of Zipangu. The other ships, which, not being so near to the land, did not suffer from the storm, and in which the two chiefs were embarked, together with the principal officers, or those whose rank entitled them to command a hundred thousand or ten thousand men, directed their course homewards, and returned to the grand khan. Those of the Tartars who remained upon the island where they were wrecked, and who amounted to about thirty thousand men, finding themselves left without shipping, abandoned by their leaders, and having neither arms nor provisions, expected nothing less than to become captives or to perish; especially as the island afforded no habitations where they could take shelter and refresh themselves. As soon as the gale ceased and the sea became smooth and calm, the people from the main island of Zipangu came over with a large force, in numerous boats, in order to make prisoners of these shipwrecked Tartars, and having landed, proceeded in search of them, but in a straggling, disorderly manner. The Tartars, on their part, acted with prudent circumspection, and, being concealed from view by some high land in the centre of the island, whilst the enemy were hurrying in pursuit of them by one road, made a circuit of the coast by another, which brought them to the place where the fleet of boats was at anchor. Finding these all abandoned, but with their colours flying, they instantly seized them and pushing off from the island, stood for the principal city of Zipangu, into which, from the appearance of the colours, they were suffered to enter unmolested. Here they found few of the inhabitants besides women, whom they retained for their own use, and drove out all others. When the king was apprised of what had taken place, he was much afflicted, and immediately gave directions for a strict blockade of the city, which was so effectual that not any person was suffered to enter or to escape from it, during six months that the siege continued. At the expiration of this time, the Tartars, despairing of succour, surrendered upon the condition of their lives being spared. These events took place in the course of the year 1264. The grand khan having learned some years after that the unfortunate issue of the expedition was to be attributed to the dissension between the two commanders, caused the head of one of them to be cut off; the other he sent to the savage island of Zorza, where it is the custom to execute criminals in the following manner. They are wrapped round both arms, in the hide of a buffalo fresh taken from the beast, which is sewed tight. As this dries, it compresses the body to such a degree that the sufferer is incapable of moving or in any manner helping himself, and thus miserably perishes.

In this island of Zipangu and the others in its vicinity, their idols are fashioned in a variety of shapes, some of them having the heads of oxen, some of swine, of dogs, goats, and many other animals. Some exhibit the appearance of a single head, with two countenances; others of three heads, one of them in its proper place, and one upon each shoulder. Some have four arms, others ten, and some an hundred; those which have the greatest number being regarded as the most powerful, and therefore entitled to the most particular worship. When they are asked by Christians wherefore they give to their deities these diversified forms, they answer that their fathers did so before them. "Those who preceded us," they say, "left them such, and such shall we transmit them to our posterity." The various ceremonies practised before these idols are so wicked and diabolical that it would be nothing less than impiety and an abomination to give an account of them in this our book. The reader should, however, be informed that the idolatrous inhabitants of these islands, when they seize the person of an enemy who has not the means of effecting his ransom for money, invite to their house all their relations and friends, and putting their prisoner to death, dress and eat the body, in a convivial manner, asserting that human flesh surpasses every other in the excellence of its flavour.

An Epic for the Conqueror

In song and story the poets of the day told of the greatness of the East and, by reflection, of the even greater might of those who would conquer in the name of their God, their state, or their language. One of the great epic poems of the sixteenth century was written by Luiz Vaz de Camões, a Portuguese of Galician descent. Camões was sent to Ceuta, on the African coast opposite Gibraltar, in *c*1547, where he lost an eye in battle; in 1553 he sailed for India, where he lived in Goa, which he hated, and engaged in expeditions against Ormuz. From there he went to the Malabar coast, which he apparently liked. Two years later Camões was at Cape Guardafui, in what is now Somalia (East Africa); in 1556 he was sent to Macão, on the China coast. He travelled widely, seeing much of the Portuguese overseas empire, and he wanted to write an epic poem to record the deeds of those he had seen in action. At some point his plan changed, and he modeled his account upon the exploits of Vasco da Gama. We do not know precisely when the result—*The Lusiads*—was written, but Camões had it, or portions of it, with him when he was wrecked at the mouth of the Mekong in 1559. He served (and was jailed) in Goa again, passed two years in Mozambique, and ultimately returned to Lisbon, to publish his poem in 1572. The following is from the first and seventh books of *The Lusiads*.

From *The Lusiads of Luiz de Camões*, trans. Leonard Bacon (New York: The Hispanic Society of America, 1950), pp. 3, 249-50. Reprinted by permission of The Hispanic Society of America.

Arms, and those matchless chiefs who from the shore
Of Western Lusitania began
To track the oceans none had sailed before,
Yet past Tapróbané's[1] far limit ran,
And daring every danger, every war,
With courage that excelled the powers of Man,
Amid remotest nations caused to rise
Young empire which they carried to the skies;

So, too, good memory of those kings who went
Afar, religion and our rule to spread;
And who, through either hateful continent,
Afric or Asia, like destruction sped;
And theirs, whose valiant acts magnificent
Saved them from the dominion of the dead,
My song shall sow through the world's every part,
So help me this my genius and my art.

---

[1] [Greek name for Ceylon.]

Of the wise Greek, no more the tale unfold,
Or the Trojan, and great voyages they made.
Of Philip's son and Trajan, leave untold
Triumphant fame in wars which they essayed.
I sing the Lusian spirit bright and bold,
That Mars and Neptune equally obeyed.
Forget all the Muse sang in ancient days,
For valor nobler yet is now to praise.

      *   *   *

I say to you, O Lusian generation,
Yours in this world is but a little place,
Not in this world, but in His congregation.
Whose rule doth the round firmament embrace;
You, in whom risk quelled not determination
Wholly to subjugate a loathsome race,
Or greed, or an allegiance incomplete
To Her Whose Essence hath in Heaven Her seat;

You Portuguese, so strong, though you are few,
Who your weak powers never stop to weigh,
Who, though you pay the price of death, ensue
The law of life that shall endure for aye,
Such was the die which Heaven cast for you,
That, be your numbers little as they may,
For Christendom you act a mighty part.
So dost Thou, Christ, exalt the meek in heart!

      *   *   *

Look on the proud herd of the Germans there,
Who in their vast plains find their nourishment,
And, in rebellion against Peter's heir,
Seek a new shepherd, a new sect invent.[2]
Look on the hideous wars to which they fare
(For with blind error they are not content),
Not against the Ottoman full up of pride,
But the Pope's sovereign power to set aside.

See the hard Englishman, who King by right
Of the divine old city claims to be,
Which town is ruled by the vile Ishmaelite.
How far vain honor is from verity!
Amid his northern snows he seeks delight
And Christian in a novel sense is he,
Against Christ's men drawing the naked brand.
But not for the reconquest of Christ's land.

[2] [A reference, of course, to Martin Luther.]

In Praise of the Settler

Poets praised not only the conqueror but also those who followed to settle, exploit, and remake the new lands. On the whole, permanent European settlement seemed unwise in tropical regions, both because the notion that white men could not work, or even long survive, under tropical conditions was a strong one, to become stronger by the nineteenth century, and because such regions already had a large labor supply. Settlers, therefore, were encouraged to go to the temperate zones of the earth, to North America, to Australasia, and to southern Africa. They were the successors to those who merely came, saw, and recorded the wonders of the new lands and were, in turn, succeeded by native-born colonials, who developed the first British empire, which was based on the principles of mercantilism. These white men pressed back (and in Tasmania exterminated) aboriginal peoples. Rudyard Kipling, the Camões of the late nineteenth and early twentieth centuries, would sing the song of the "white Dominions," of Canada, Australia, New Zealand, and South Africa, while showing how the ties that bound the empire together—commerce, language, assumptions of race (or "stock"), and religion ("The Abbey makes us We")—continued to operate except for that breakaway portion that had become the United States. The following poem, "The Native-Born," was written by Kipling in 1894.

From *Rudyard Kipling's Verse* (Garden City: Doubleday & Company, Inc., 1924), pp. 105–7. Reprinted by permission of Mrs. George Bambridge, Macmillan & Co., Ltd., the Macmillan Company of Canada, and Doubleday & Company, Inc.

We've drunk to the Queen—God bless her!—
　　We've drunk to our mother's land;
We've drunk to our English brother,
　　(But he does not understand);
We've drunk to the wide creation,
　　And the Cross swings low for the morn,
Last toast, and of Obligation,
　　A health to the Native-born!

They change their skies above them,
　　But not their hearts that roam!
We learned from our wistful mothers
　　To call old England "home";
We read of the English sky-lark,
　　Of the spring in the English lanes,
But we screamed with the painted lories

As we rode on the dusty plains!
They passed with their old-world legends—
   Their tales of wrong and dearth—
Our fathers held by purchase,
   But we by the right of birth;
Our heart's where they rocked our cradle,
   Our love where we spent our toil,
And our faith and our hope and our honour
   We pledge to our native soil!

I charge you charge your glasses—
   I charge you drink with me
To the men of the Four New Nations,
   And the Islands of the Sea—
To the last least lump of coral
   That none may stand outside,
And our own good pride shall teach us
   To praise our comrade's pride!

To the hush of the breathless morning
   On the thin, tin, crackling roofs,
To the haze of the burned back-ranges
   And the dust of the shoeless hoofs—
To the risk of a death by drowning,
   To the risk of a death by drouth—
To the men of a million acres,
   To the Sons of the Golden South!

To the Sons of the Golden South (Stand up!),
   And the life we live and know,
Let a fellow sing o' the little things he cares about,
If a fellow fights for the little things he cares about
   With the weight of a single blow!

To the smoke of a hundred coasters,
   To the sheep on a thousand hills,
To the sun that never blisters,
   To the rain that never chills—
To the land of the waiting springtime,
   To our five-meal, meat-fed men,
To the tall, deep-bosomed women,
   And the children nine and ten!

And the children nine and ten (Stand up!),
   And the life we live and know,
Let a fellow sing o' the little things he cares about,
If a fellow fights for the little things he cares about
   With the weight of a two-fold blow!

To the far-flung fenceless prairie
   Where the quick cloud-shadows trail,
To our neighbor's barn in the offing
   And the line of the new-cut rail;

To the plough in her league-long furrow
  With the grey Lake gulls behind—
To the weight of a half-year's winter
  And the warm wet western wind!

To the home of the floods and thunder,
  To her pale dry healing blue—
To the lift of the great Cape combers,
  And the smell of the baked Karroo.
To the growl of the sluicing stamp-head—
  To the reef and the water-gold,
To the last and the largest Empire,
  To the map that is half unrolled!

To our dear dark foster-mothers,
  To the heathen songs they sung—
To the heathen speech we babbled
  Ere we came to the white man's tongue.
To the cool of our deep verandas—
  To the blaze of our jewelled main,
To the night, to the palms in the moonlight,
  And the fire-fly in the cane!

To the hearth of Our People's People—
  To her well-ploughed windy sea,
To the hush of our dread high-altar
  Where The Abbey makes us We.
To the grist of the slow-ground ages,
  To the gain that is yours and mine
To the Bank of the Open Credit,
  To the Power-house of the Line!

The East Replies to the West

In 1681 the powerful Louis XIV, the Sun King of France, dispatched a letter to the King of Tonkin, in southeast Asia. Carried by an emissary from the French Society of Foreign Missions, the letter never reached Tonkin's ruler, Chua Trinh-Tac, who refused to accept it and who died while Louis's messenger was seeking an audience. Chua Trinh-Tac's successor also refused to grant an audience to the Frenchman, but he sent a reply to Louis which was in no way inferior to that which had been sent by his "dear and good friend," who had proposed to supply advisors to Tonkin—a not uncommon, and often unintentional, form of early imperialism.

From Georges Taboulet, ed., *La geste française en Indochine* (Paris, 1955), I, 84–86, and in English trans. by Margaret W. Broekhuysen in Harry J. Benda and John A. Larkin, eds., *The World of Southeast Asia* (New York, 1967). Copyright by M. Taboulet, Adrien-Maisonneuve of Paris, and Harper & Row, Inc., New York.

Most high, most excellent, most mighty and most magnanimous Prince, our very dear and good friend, may it please God to increase your greatness with a happy end!

We hear from our subjects who were in your Realm what protection you accorded them. We appreciate this all the more since we have for you all the esteem that one can have for a prince as illustrious through his military valor as he is commendable for the justice which he exercises in his Realm. We have even been informed that you have not been satisfied to extend this general protection to our subjects but, in particular, that you gave effective proofs of it to Messrs. Deydier and de Bourges. We would have wished that they might have been able to recognize all the favors they received from you by having presents worthy of you offered you; but since the war which we have had for several years, in which all of Europe had banded together against us, prevented our vessels from going to the Indies, at the present time, when we are at peace after having gained many victories and expanded our Realm through the conquest of several important places, we have immediately given orders to the Royal Company to establish itself in your kingdom as soon as possible, and have commanded Messrs. Deydier and de Bourges to remain with you in order to maintain a good relationship between our subjects and yours, also to warn us on occasions that might present themselves when we might be able to give you proofs of our esteem and of our wish to concur with your satisfaction as well as with your best interests.

17

By way of initial proof, we have given orders to have brought to you some presents which we believe might be agreeable to you. But the one thing in the world which we desire most, both for you and for your Realm, would be to obtain for your subjects who have already embraced the law of the only true God of heaven and earth, the freedom to profess it, since this law is the highest, the noblest, the most sacred and especially the most suitable to have kings reign absolutely over the people.

We are even quite convinced that, if you knew the truths and the maxims which it teaches, you would give first of all to your subjects the glorious example of embracing it. We wish you this incomparable blessing together with a long and happy reign, and we pray God that it may please Him to augment your greatness with the happiest of endings.

Written at Saint-Germain-en-Laye, the 10th day of January, 1681,

Your very dear and good friend,

Louis

The King of Tonkin sends to the King of France a letter to express to him his best sentiments, saying that he was happy to learn that fidelity is a durable good of man and that justice is the most important of things. Consequently practicing of fidelity and justice cannot but yield good results. Indeed, though France and our Kingdom differ as to mountains, rivers, and boundaries, if fidelity and justice reign among our villages, our conduct will express all of our good feelings and contain precious gifts. Your communication, which comes from a country which is a thousand leagues away, and which proceeds from the heart as a testimony of your sincerity, merits repeated consideration and infinite praise. Politeness toward strangers is nothing unusual in our country. There is not a stranger who is not well received by us. How then could we refuse a man from France, which is the most celebrated among the kingdoms of the world and which for love of us wishes to frequent us and bring us merchandise? These feelings of fidelity and justice are truly worthy to be applauded. As regards your wish that we should cooperate in propagating your religion, we do not dare to permit it, for there is an ancient custom, introduced by edicts, which formally forbids it. Now, edicts are promulgated only to be carried out faithfully; without fidelity nothing is stable. How could we disdain a well-established custom to satisfy a private friendship? . . .

We beg you to understand well that this is our communication concerning our mutual acquaintance. This then is my letter. We send you herewith a modest gift which we offer you with a glad heart.

This letter was written at the beginning of winter and on a beautiful day.

The Splendor of Decay

India was long known to the West and Africa had begun to emerge from its "darkness" when Henri Mouhot, a young French Protestant under English sponsorship, rediscovered the lost and ancient Khmer civilization at Angkor Wat and Angkor Thom. Married to an English girl who was related to the great British explorer of Africa, Mungo Park, Mouhot wanted to investigate Siam. Leaving his wife in London, he set off for Bangkok in 1858, travelled extensively in Siam and Cambodia, and in 1860 spent three weeks at Angkor examining the great ruins. The following year he died of fever near Louang Prabang, and in 1864 Madame Mouhot saw published in England the diaries her husband had compiled. This edition, and a magazine publication in France the year before, caught the imagination of the Western world, for here was that most romantic of all wonders of the East, a Shangri-la, a rose-red city of Petra, a lost civilization in a remote corner of the globe. Mouhot, who lies buried on a Laotian hillside under a gravestone six years in error as to his death-date, had dramatically furthered the next step in exploration, the step by which Kajaraho, Polunnaruwa, Zimbabwe, Macchu Picchu, Chichen-Itza, and Nineveh would all become real once again.

From *Henri Mouhot's Diary: Travels in the Central Parts of Siam, Cambodia and Laos during the Years 1858–61*, abridged and edited by Christopher Pym (Kuala Lumpur: Oxford University Press, 1966), pp. 81–85. Reprinted by permission of the East Asian Branch of Oxford University Press.

The entrance to the great lake of Cambodia is grand and beautiful. The river becomes wider and wider, until at last it is four or five miles in breadth; and then you enter the immense sheet of water called Tonli-Sap, as large and full of motion as a sea. It is more than 120 miles long, and must be at least 400 in circumference.

The shore is low, and thickly covered with trees, which are half submerged; and in the distance is visible an extensive range of mountains whose highest peaks seem lost in the clouds. The waves glitter in the broad sunshine with a brilliancy which the eye can scarcely support, and, in many parts of the lake, nothing is visible all around but water. In the centre is planted a tall mast, indicating the boundary between the kingdoms of Siam and Cambodia. . . .

Nokhor, or Ongcor, was the capital of the ancient kingdom of Cambodia, or Khmer, formerly so famous among the great states of Indo-China, that almost the only tradition preserved in the country mentions that empire as having had twenty kings who paid tribute to it, as having kept up an army of five or six million soldiers, and that the buildings of the royal treasury occupied a space of more than 300 miles.

In the province still bearing the name of Ongcor . . . there are on the banks of the Mekon . . . ruins of such grandeur, remains of structures which must have been raised at such an immense cost of labour, that, at the first view, one is filled with profound admiration, and cannot but ask what has become of this powerful race, so civilised, so enlightened, the authors of these gigantic works?

One of these temples—a rival to that of Solomon, and erected by some ancient Michael Angelo—might take an honourable place beside our most beautiful buildings. It is grander than anything left to us by Greece or Rome, and presents a sad contrast to the state of barbarism in which the nation is now plunged.

Unluckily the scourge of war, aided by time, the great destroyer, who respects nothing, and perhaps also by earthquakes, has fallen heavily on the greater part of the other monuments; and the work of destruction and decay continues among those which still remain standing, imposing, and majestic, amidst the masses of ruins all around.

One seeks in vain for any historical souvenirs of the many kings who must have succeeded one another on the throne of the powerful empire of Maha-Nocor-Khmer. There exists a tradition of a leprous king, to whom is attributed the commencement of the great temple, but all else is totally forgotten. The inscriptions, with which some of the columns are covered, are illegible; and, if you interrogate the Cambodians as to the founders of Ongcor-Wat, you invariably receive one of these four replies: "It is the work of Pra-Eun, the king of the angels"; "It is the work of the giants"; "It was built by the leprous king"; or else, "It made itself." . . .

It is remarkable that none of these monuments were intended for habitations; all were temples of Buddhism. The statues and bas-reliefs, however, curiously enough, represent entirely secular subjects—monarchs surrounded by their wives, their heads and arms loaded with ornaments. . . . On a sort of esplanade is a statue, said to be that of the leprous king. It is a little above the middle height, and the prince is seated in a noble and dignified attitude. The head, particularly, is a *chef d'œuvre,* the features perfectly regular, and possessing a manly beauty of a description seen now in very rare instances, and only amongst Cambodians of unmixed race. . . .

. . . [T]he temple of Ongcor, the most beautiful and best preserved of all the remains, . . . is also the first which presents itself to the eye of the traveller, making him forget all the fatigues of the journey, filling him with admiration and delight, such as would be experienced on finding a verdant oasis in the sandy desert. Suddenly, and as if by enchantment, he seems to be transported from barbarism to civilisation, from profound darkness to light. . . .

Romance of the Jungle

The mountains, the deserts, and the dense forests of the newly discovered lands set Europe apart from the lost cities, the ancient civilizations, and the peoples of Africa, South America, the Pacific, and the East. Europeans—in particular French and British travellers —were as fascinated with the strange new landscapes as with the people they found. That West Africa was a "white man's graveyard" was thought to result as much from its dense, jungle coverage as from the fevers that arose there. The British, especially, were fascinated by the tropics, and their commercial empire, as distinct from their empire of settlement, was largely tropical. In 1907 W. George (later Sir George) Maxwell, a British naturalist, wrote perceptively of the reality and of the myth of the jungle in his book, *In Malay Forests*. Even today men on patrol in the Thai-Malaysian border regions find that they require as much as seven days to move four miles; in the nineteenth and early twentieth centuries, when equipment was heavier and less sophisticated, progress often was slower. Thus, the Western perception of time, of movement, of performance, and of life had to adjust to the new environments. One such adjustment lay in coming to terms with the new landscapes of the empire, something few expatriates were ever able to do.

From *In Malay Forests* by Sir George Maxwell (Edinburgh: William Blackwood & Sons, Ltd., 1907), pp. 1–8. Reprinted by permission of the publisher.

It is almost the literal truth that the whole peninsula is covered with forest. It is not that the country is uninhabited, for it has a population of some hundreds of thousands: but it is that the inhabited area, every yard of which has been won from, and hacked out of the forest, is infinitesimal in comparison with the extent of the forest that remains untouched.

Throughout its hundreds of miles of length and breadth the Malay Peninsula is practically one vast forest. The great alluvial tin-fields of Kinta, Larut, Selangor, and Seremban, where tens of thousands of Chinese coolies strip the surface to lay bare the ore, are really mere patches; and the towns, palatial and magnificent though the buildings of some of them are, are nothing more than specks in an expanse that sweeps from one Sultanate to another, and is only limited by the sea. . . . It is, however, difficult at first to realise the environment of the forest. When the newcomer has left his steamer, and the railway has taken him to the town which is his destination, it is possible that he may fail to appreciate the most wonderful of all the new sights around him; he may, and most frequently does, accept the dense mass of trees and vegetation that shuts in the railway line as "the jungle," and consider the timber-clad mountains merely in the light of scenery.

In a Malay village one may better realise the manner in which the forest hems in the cultivated area. The settlement is generally situated on the banks of a river. By the water's edge are the houses, built under the shade of fruit-trees, and behind them are the flat, irrigated padifields. On all sides this area is shut in by a dark heavy line that uprears itself, around and above it, like the walls of a prison. This line is the forest edge; and thence the forest spreads in every direction, miles upon miles, until some other village is reached; there it opens out again, and sweeping round the clearing, as a wave encircles some ocean rock, closes in again behind it and continues, over mountains, over plains, until the sea is reached.

But it is when he views it from a mountain peak that the stranger can best see the extent of the forest. He will then discover, what the Malay can never for a minute forget, that he lives his life in the midst of a forest which is as much apart from him as it is around him. The fact that it extends, interminable, far beyond the horizon on every side, then for the first time makes its indelible impression upon his mind.

This other wonderful thing he will perhaps first realise: the forest is an evergreen; the season, whose changes in the cultivated area turn brown soil to the tender green of the young padi shoots, to the richness of the colour of the swelling plants, and to the golden wealth of the ripened grain, fails to touch the forest. Neither the season, nor the flight of time, leaves a mark upon the forest; virgin in the days of which we cannot guess the morn, virgin in our days, virgin it will remain in the days of generations yet unborn.

On the slopes of the nearest spur each individual tree stands clear, each giant form showing the swelling roundness of its wealth of bough and leaf. Tier upon tier, the trees stand thickly massed, without a break, from the level of the plain to the height of the topmost trees that show their heads against the sky-line. Deep, dark, sombre green is the colour of this near range; here and there one may catch glimpses of lighter shades, a few scattered patches perhaps of sage green where some trees, after fruiting, are putting forth a new flush of leaves; possibly there may be a speck of vivid red that marks a tree whose young shoots assume an unusual colour. But the contrast only accentuates the prevailing tone. . . .

. . . [S]o deep, so soft is the mantle of forest, that you may fail to realise the grandeur of the mountains. They have not the austerity that belongs to nakedness. To right and to left, where the mountain spurs run out and down to the plain, your eyes rest on slopes which, though steep perhaps, are softly undulating. Each tree melts gently into its neighbour, or partly hides it; all is green and harmonious, and the mountain offers a face which appears to be as smooth and unbroken as a pasture land. But sometimes you may see how deceptive this appearance is. It has been raining, and a great cloud comes slowly swimming landward from the sea. The direction that it takes will bring it within a mile of you. As it approaches the mountain you wonder what will happen,—whether it will rest against the mountainside, or whether it will roll upwards through the trees. But to your amazement, when the cloud edge touches the mountain it does not stop. Then you see that the whole cloud is swimming on into the mountain. What has happened is that a mountain ravine has acted as the channel up which a current of air is rushing skywards from the plain, and into the ravine the cloud is being slowly sucked. As the cloud enters, its shape and size and colour help your eye to see both sides of the ravine, and you may vaguely estimate the depth and width of the valley that had been strangely invisible although so close. But as soon as the cloud is past and gone, the trees on both sides of the ravine seem to leap together; and, though you now know exactly where to look, waving branches and woven leaves defy your efforts to say where the entrance is. You then wonder how many similar places are hidden around you, and picture to yourself the great sea cloud hemmed in by the sides of the ravine and still swimming farther landward. . . .

But come down from the mountain peak, and walk alone along a forest path. Though it is midday it is very sombre. The sun cannot pierce the dense foliage of the branches of the giant trees, and so heavily do shadows lie upon shadows that the very green seems almost black. The sheltered air is fresh and cool, and there is an almost perfect stillness. Underfoot, except where the path is trodden bare, is a matting of dead leaves and of sweet damp moss. The track upon which you stand is a foot or perhaps a foot and a half wide, and at the height of your body the width of the open way is perhaps three feet. The daily passage of the Malays keeps back the encroachment of brambles and forest creepers. But the track is only wide enough and the opening only high enough to allow a man to pass. You could not ride even the smallest and handiest of ponies along it.

To right and left of the path the forest appears to be almost impenetrable. The trees grow so thickly together that you are closed in by a small but unbroken circle of tree-trunks. Between the trees there are tangled masses of bushes, briers, and saplings. Rattans and creepers of every kind crawl along the ground and among the trees, sometimes hanging in heavy festoons and sometimes tense with the pressure that they exert. So thick and strong is the mass of creepers that when a wood-cutter has hacked through a tree-trunk it is often kept upright by the ligaments that bind it to the surrounding trees.

After an hour's walk along a forest path, a casual observer might say that, so far as he could see, the forest contained no flowers, no butterflies, no birds, no life of any kind. But if you sit upon a fallen tree-trunk and look around, you may see a little more. High in a tree, and almost out of sight, you may see an occasional flower, and lower down perhaps, your eye may light upon an inconspicuous spray of blossoms that a careful scrutiny shows to be a miniature orchid. There are few butterflies in the forest, but now and then, if you are by one of the openings among the trees, which are to the winged creatures what the paths are to us, you may see a moth or butterfly pass by flapping its heavy velvet wings. You seldom hear a bird, but if you are quiet and wait long enough some tiny sun-bird may come your way, or, perhaps some weird bird with light-blue eyes and an enormous tail; or a jungle-hen may creep out from under a bush, and scratch for ants' eggs in an open space where a tree has fallen. The only other thing that you will see, except an occasional lizard, will be ants, and perhaps a millepede. If you know where to look for them, you will see the tracks of four-footed animals, but you will not see the animals themselves.

But in a forest which you know to be so vast and so boundless you have a right to expect more than you have seen. Ants, a butterfly, even a bird, do not and cannot represent the life of this great gloomy place. But more you cannot see. You are the centre of a small circle whose radius varies from fifteen to thirty yards. Inside this circle you can see more or less distinctly; outside it everything is hidden. Even so huge an animal as an elephant is sometimes invisible at fifteen yards, and almost always invisible at thirty yards. Wherever you go you carry with you that little circle outside which lies the unknown. The path that lies behind you is, as soon as it passes outside that circle, as full of the unknown as the path before you or the tangle on either side. So little do you see that the feeling comes over you that you are alone in the midst of mysterious, hidden things. The feeling that immediately follows this is that these mysterious things are not merely hidden, but are specially hidden from you. . . .

At all times you may see things happen of which the reason is hard to divine. Though not a breath of air can be felt to move, a frond of a palm may begin to sway gently and rhythmically backwards and forwards while all the other fronds of the same tree remain as motion-less as the trees around. You examine the palm to see if there is possibly a rat or some other animal at its base, but can discover nothing. Sometimes one single leaf amidst the numbers on a branch may begin without apparent cause to be violently agitated, and will as suddenly stop.

The Malays always consider themselves as intruders when they enter the forest, and never forget their awe of and reverence for it.

They seldom go into the forest alone; and when one man asks another to accompany him, the reason that he is going into the forest is always considered to be sufficient in itself. While it is true that the forest lies almost at their doors, they never forget not merely that no man knows its extent, but that it actually is without bound or limit. . . .

The Native People

While the forest knew no bounds, people did, and in the colonies of settlement the indigenous populations—North American Indians, Australian aborigines, Hottentots—were pressed back from the coasts, controlled, and often decimated by the whites swarming out from the metropolitan centers of empire. The native people were objects of fear when they stood and fought; when they did not, they were subjects for curiosity. The following account, from Watkin Tench's narrative of the settlement of Port Jackson and Botany Bay in 1788, tells of how the whites approached the natives of New South Wales. It also reveals something of the values by which the settlers judged the natives: those skills they respected, what they took to be proper standards of beauty, and notions relating to how the aborigines were to be approached. The conventional wisdom of the day helped limit interracial sexual relations, but this changed in time and, in any case, did not prevail in many other portions of the European empires, giving rise to *lançado, mestizo,* mulatto, and Eurasian classes.

From *A Narrative of the Expedition to Botany Bay . . .* by Watkin Tench (London: J. Debrett, 1789, pp. 89–96.)

. . . [W]e had been but a very few days at Port Jackson, when an alteration in the behaviour of the natives was perceptible; and I wish I could add, that a longer residence in their neighbourhood had introduced a greater degree of cordiality and intermixture between the old, and new, lords of the soil, than at the day on which this publication is dated subsists. From their easy reception of us in the beginning, many were induced to call in question the accounts which Mr. [James] Cook had given of this people. That celebrated navigator, we were willing to believe, had somehow by his conduct offended them, which prevented the intercourse that would otherwise have taken place. The result, however, of our repeated endeavours to induce them to come among us has been such as to confirm me in an opinion, that they either fear or despise us too much, to be anxious for a closer connection. And I beg leave at once, to apprize the reader, that all I can here, or in any future part of this work, relate with fidelity of the natives of New South Wales, must be made up of detached observations, taken at different times, and not from a regular series of knowledge of the customs and manners of a people, with whom opportunities of communication are so scarce, as to have been seldom obtained.

In their persons, they are far from being a stout race of men, though nimble, sprightly, and vigorous. The deficiency of one of the fore teeth of the upper jaw, mentioned by [William] Dampier, we have seen in almost the whole of the men; but their organs of sight, so far from being defective, as that author mentions those of the inhabitants of the western side of the continent to be, are remarkably quick and piercing. Their colour, Mr. Cook is inclined to think rather a deep chocolate, than an absolute black, though he confesses, they have the appearance of the latter, which he attributes to the greasy filth their skins are loaded with. Of their want of cleanliness we have had sufficient proofs, but I am of opinion, all the washing in the world would not render them two degrees less black than an African negro. At some of our first interviews, we had several droll instances of their mistaking the Africans we brought with us for their own countrymen.

Notwithstanding the disregard they have invariably shewn for all the finery we could deck them with, they are fond of adorning themselves with scars, which increase their natural hideousness. It is hardly possible to see any thing in human shape more ugly, than one of these savages thus scarified, and farther ornamented with a fish bone struck through the gristle of the nose. The custom of daubing themselves with white earth is also frequent among both sexes: but, unlike the inhabitants of the islands in the Pacific Ocean, they reject the beautiful feathers which the birds of their country afford.

Exclusive of their weapons of offence, and a few stone hatchets very rudely fashioned, their ingenuity is confined to manufacturing small nets, in which they put the fish they catch, and to fish-hooks made of bone, neither of which are unskilfully executed. On many of the rocks are also to be found delineations of the figures of men and birds, very poorly cut.

Of the use or benefit of cloathing, these people appear to have no comprehension, though their sufferings from the climate they live in, strongly point out the necessity of a covering from the rigour of the seasons. Both sexes, and those of all ages, are invariably found naked. But it must not be inferred from this, that custom so inures them to the changes of the elements, as to make them bear with indifference the extremes of heat and cold; for we have had visible and repeated proofs, that the latter affects them severely, when they are seen shivering, and huddling themselves up in heaps in their huts, or the caverns of the rocks, until a fire can be kindled.

Than these huts nothing more rude in construction, or deficient in conveniency, can be imagined. They consist only of pieces of bark laid together in the form of an oven, open at one end, and very low, though long enough for a man to lie at full length in. There is reason, however, to believe, that they depend less on them for shelter, than on the caverns with which the rocks abound.

To cultivation of the ground they are utter strangers, and wholly depend for food on the few fruits they gather; the roots they dig up in the swamps; and the fish they pick up along shore, or contrive to strike from their canoes with spears. Fishing, indeed, seems to engross nearly the whole of their time, probably from its forming the chief part of a subsistence, which, observation has convinced us, nothing short of the most painful labour, and unwearied assiduity can procure. When fish are scarce, which frequently happens, they often watch the moment of our hauling the seine, and have more than once been known to plunder its contents, in spite of the opposition of those on the spot to guard it: and this even after having received a part of what had been caught. The only resource at these times is to shew a musquet, and if the bare sight is not sufficient, to fire it over their heads, which has seldom failed of dispersing them hitherto, but how long the terror which it excites may continue is doubtful.

The canoes in which they fish are as despicable as their huts, being nothing more than a large piece of bark tied up at both ends with vines. Their dexterous management of them, added to the swiftness with which they paddle, and the boldness that leads them several miles in the open sea, are, nevertheless, highly deserving of admiration. A canoe is seldom seen without a fire in it, to dress the fish by, as soon as caught: fire they procure by attrition.

From their manner of disposing of those who die . . . as well as from every other observation, there seems no reason to suppose these people cannibals; nor do they ever eat animal substances in a raw state, unless pressed by extreme hunger, but indiscriminately broil them, and their vegetables, on a fire, which renders these last an innocent food, though in their raw state many of them are of a poisonous quality: as a poor convict who unguardedly ate of them experienced, by falling a sacrifice in twenty-four hours afterwards. If bread be given to the Indians, they chew and spit it out again, seldom choosing to swallow it. Salt beef and pork they like rather better, but spirits they never could be brought to taste a second time.

The only domestic animal they have is the dog, which in their language is called Dingo, and a good deal resembles the fox dog of England. These animals are equally shy of us, and attached to the natives. One of them is now in the possession of the Governor, and tolerably well reconciled to his new master. As the Indians see the dislike of the dogs to us, they are sometimes mischievous enough to set them on single persons whom they chance to meet in the woods. A surly fellow was one day out shooting, when the natives attempted to divert themselves in this manner at his expence. The man bore the teazing and gnawing of the dog at his heels for some time, but apprehending at length, that his patience might embolden them to use still farther liberties, he turned round and shot poor Dingo dead on the spot: the owners of him set off with the utmost expedition.

There is no part of the behaviour of these people, that has puzzled us more, than that which relates to their women. Comparatively speaking we have seen but few of them, and those have been sometimes kept back with every symptom of jealous sensibility; and sometimes offered with every appearance of courteous familiarity. Cautious, however, of alarming the feelings of the men on so tender a point, we have constantly made a rule of treating the females with that distance and reserve, which we judged most likely to remove any impression they might have received of our intending ought, which could give offence on so delicate a subject. And so successful have our endeavours been, that a quarrel on this head has in no instance, that I know of, happened. The tone of voice of the women, which is pleasingly soft and feminine, forms a striking contrast to the rough guttural pronunciation of the men. Of the other charms of the ladies I shall be silent, though justice obliges me to mention, that, in the opinion of some amongst us, they shew a degree of timidity and bashfulness, which are, perhaps, inseparable from the female character in its rudest state. It is not a little singular, that the custom of cutting off the two lower joints of the little finger of the left hand, observed in the Society Islands, is found here among the women, who have for the most part undergone this amputation. Hitherto we have not been able to trace out the cause of this usage. At first we supposed it to be peculiar to the married women, or those who have borne children; but this conclusion must have been erroneous, as we have no right to believe that celibacy prevails in any instance, and some of the oldest women are without this distinction; and girls of a very tender age are marked by it.

On first setting foot in the country, we were inclined to hold the spears of the natives very cheap. Fatal experience has, however, convinced us, that the wound inflicted by this weapon is not a trivial one; and that the skill of the Indians in throwing it, is far from despicable. Besides more than a dozen convicts who have unaccountably disappeared, we know that two, who were employed as rush cutters up the harbour, were (from what cause we are yet ignorant) most dreadfully mangled and butchered by the natives. A spear had passed entirely through the thickest part of the body of one of them, though a very robust man, and the skull of the other was beaten in. Their tools were taken away, but some provisions which they had with them at the time of the murder, and the cloaths, were left untouched. In addition to this misfortune, two more convicts, who were peaceably engaged in picking of greens, on a spot very remote from that where their comrades suffered, were unawares attacked by a party of Indians, and before they could effect their escape, one of them was pierced by a spear in the hip, after which they knocked him down, and plundered his cloaths. The poor wretch, though dreadfully wounded, made shift to crawl off, but his companion was carried away by these barbarians, and his fate doubtful, until a soldier, a few days afterwards, picked up his jacket and hat in a native's hut, the latter pierced through by a spear. We have found that these spears are not made invariably alike, some of them being barbed like a fish gig, and others simply pointed. In repairing them they are no less dextrous than in throwing them. A broken one being given by a gentleman to an Indian, he instantly snatched up an oyster-shell, and converted it with his teeth into a tool, with which he presently fashioned the spear, and rendered it fit for use: in performing this operation, the sole of his foot served him as a workboard. Nor are their weapons of offence confined to the spear only, for they have besides long wooden swords, shaped like a sabre, capable of inflicting a mortal wound, and clubs of an immense size. Small targets, made of the bark of trees, are likewise now and then to be seen among them.

From circumstances which have been observed, we have sometimes been inclined to believe these people at war with each other. They have more than once been seen assembled, as if bent on an expedition. An officer one day met fourteen of them marching along in a regular Indian file through the woods, each man armed with a spear in his right hand, and a large stone in his left: at their head appeared a chief, who was distinguished by being painted. Though in the proportion of five to one of our people they passed peaceably on.

That their skill in throwing the spear sometimes enables them to kill the kangaroo we have no right to doubt, as a long splinter of this weapon was taken out of the thigh of one of these animals, over which the flesh had completely closed; but we have never discovered that they have any method of ensnaring them, or that they know any other beasts but the kangaroo and dog. Whatever animal is shown them, a dog excepted, they call kangaroo: a strong presumption that the wild animals of the country are very few.

Soon after our arrival at Port Jackson, I was walking out near a place where I observed a party of Indians, busily employed in looking at some sheep in an inclosure, and repeatedly crying out, Kangaroo, kangaroo! As this seemed to afford them pleasure, I was willing to increase it by pointing out the horses and cows, which were at no great distance. But unluckily, at the moment, some female convicts, employed near the place, made their appearance, and all my endeavours to divert their attention from the ladies became fruitless. They attempted not, however, to offer them the least degree of violence or injury, but stood at the distance of several paces, expressing very significantly the manner they were attracted.

It would be trespassing on the reader's indulgence were I to impose on him an account of any civil regulations, or ordinances, which may possibly exist among this people. I declare to him, that I know not of any, and that excepting a little tributary respect which the younger part appear to pay those more advanced in years, I never could observe any degrees of subordination among them. To their religious rites and opinions I am equally a stranger. Had an opportunity offered of seeing the ceremonies observed at disposing of the dead, perhaps, some insight might have been gained; but all that we at present know with certainty is, that they burn the corpse, and afterwards heap up the earth around it, somewhat in the manner of the small tumuli, found in many counties of England. . . .

I have thus impartially stated the situation of matters, as they stand while I write, between the natives and us; that greater progress in attaching them to us has not been made, I have only to regret; but that all ranks of men have tried to effect it, by every reasonable effort from which success might have been expected, I can testify; nor can I omit saying, that in the higher stations this has been eminently conspicuous. The public orders of Governor [Arthur] Phillip have invariably tended to promote such a behavior on our side, as was most likely to produce this much wished-for event. To what cause then are we to attribute the distance which the accomplishment of it appears at? I answer, to the fickle, jealous, wavering, disposition of the people we have to deal with, who, like all other savages, are either too indolent, too indifferent, or too fearful to form an attachment on easy terms, with those who differ in habits and manners so widely from themselves.

An Asian Sees His People
Through European Eyes

Intermarriage, intermating, the heavy impress of missionary education and administrative control, and the great variety of forces with which European society was freighted changed many of the indigenous people with a speed that was remarkable. An excellent example of the ways in which perception varied from people to people, and generation to generation, arises from the *Voyage of Abdullah.* Abdullah bin Abdul Kadir was a well known *munshi,* or Malay language teacher, who in 1838 went as interpreter with two emissaries from the British government in Singapore to visit the royal state of Kelantan, where the death of the Sultan and subsequent civil war had thrown commerce into chaos. Abdullah lived well in Malacca and Singapore on his interpreter's income, and he was representative of that intermediate class of the locally-born who directly benefited from the presence of Europeans. In the extract that follows, Abdullah sees the Malays as the British saw them; the fact that he was not himself of "pure Malay blood" (for one great-grandfather had been a Yemeni Arab, a great-grandmother a Tamil of Mysore, a grandmother a Malacca Indian, and his mother was of Tamil descent) may also have accounted for the distance he put between himself and the east coast Malays among whom he travelled.

From *The Voyage of Abdullah,* trans. A. E. Coope (Singapore: Malaysia Publishing House, Ltd., 1949), pp. 15–17. Reprinted by permission of the East Asian Branch of Oxford University Press, holders of the copyright.

As we sailed I pondered again on the condition of Pahang. Why, I asked myself had a State once famous among the nations sunk to such a level of poverty and desolation? There was no obvious reason why it should have degenerated, seeing that it had not been plundered by enemies or conquered by another country.

In my opinion, this fall was not due to pirates, for I have never heard of any great country losing its trade and wealth on account of pirates. And it was not due to poverty of soil, for the soil of Pahang is very fertile.

Nor was it due merely to the laziness of the inhabitants, for there has never yet been a country anywhere in the world in which all the inhabitants were lazy; if any man who is willing to exert himself to seek fortune, knows that his enjoyment of such fortune will be undisturbed, then even if only half the population do work for their living with energy and loyalty, their country cannot fail to become great and prosperous.

No, in my opinion, the reason for the poverty of Pahang is to be found in the fact that its inhabitants live in continual fear of the oppression and cruelty of the Rajas and other notables. Naturally they feel that it is useless to be energetic when it is certain that any profits they make will be grabbed by those higher up. And so they remain poor and miserable all their lives.

Thus I made up my mind, that the reason why the people of that country could not attain peace and comfort was the badness of its government. And all the evils from which they suffered were due to the wickedness and stupidity of the Rajas. I can think of no other reason.

I reflected on the difference between the condition of the people of Pahang and of us who live in serenity under English rule. We are as good as Rajas; no one fears another and no one can oppress another. And the reason is that the administration in all its actions has one essential aim—the happiness of the people. . . .

[Upon arriving at Kuala Trengganu] I questioned the Head of the Customs. "Sir, what are the regulations and prohibitions in force here? We are new-comers and want to go to the market to get provisions and we don't know the local code."

"There is no market at this time of day," he said. "The market is held only in the evening. As regards the laws of the country, you must not keep an umbrella up when passing the house of a Raja. And you must not wear shoes or yellow clothes or fine muslin. All these are absolutely forbidden."

When I heard this, I smiled inwardly.

What stupid and pointless regulations! What piffling things were forbidden as criminal! Why didn't they forbid birds to fly over the palace? Why didn't they forbid mosquitoes to bite the Raja and bugs to hide in his pillow? Why didn't they forbid elephants to trumpet in front of the palace and people to have cock-fights in front of it? All such things are on a par with the things which are prohibited—mole-hills made into mountains!

But when it comes to prohibitions which are sensible and beneficial to mankind, nothing is said! What about the smoking of opium, which ruins people! What about all the different kinds of gambling that go on, and bad customs learned from the Chinese! There is no doubt that they ruin God's people, but they are not forbidden.

What about clothes stiff with dirt, not washed for four or five months! (Full of lice too—sit awhile and catch some lice as you sit!) That's not forbidden.

And wherever I went I saw children playing about and doing as they pleased, idling about without getting any education or doing any work. That's not forbidden.

And when a white man or other foreigner comes, hundreds of

grown-up people and children rush to crowd round, struggling for a place. And everyone leaves any work by which he might earn a living for himself and his family! Very improper and unmannerly! But that doesn't matter.

And all through the town there are puddles and rubbish and filth and undergrowth full of snakes and almost high enough to harbour tigers. But that doesn't matter!

Suppose a foreigner newly-arrived wears yellow clothes or uses an umbrella to keep the sun off his head, does that lower the Raja's dignity or harm him in any way? If it does, then it follows that, Raja's dignity and claim to respect is dependent on unimportant trifles, not on their character and reputation for justice. And it is clear that the Rajas are aware that their slackness and neglect of good government may lose them the respect and esteem of the people, so they compel them to show them honour and to exalt them in trifling matters. . . .

East and West

The following folk tale is from Japan.

From *The Fairy Tale Tree: Stories From All Over the World* retold by Vladislav Stanovsky and Jan Vladislav, translated by Jean Layton (New York: G. P. Putnam's Sons, 1961), p. 242. Copyright © 1961 by Artia. Reprinted by permission of G. P. Putnam's Sons.

Once upon a time there was a man who did nothing all day long—he just waited and hoped that suddenly he would meet with unexpected good fortune and become rich in an instant without any effort.

And thus he lived for many a year, until one day he heard tell that there was a certain island inhabited by people who had only one eye.

"At last! That will be my good fortune," thought the man to himself. "I'll travel to that island, I'll catch one of these one-eyed creatures and bring him back and show him in the market-place for a penny a look. In a short while I shall be a rich man."

And the more he thought about it, the more he liked the idea.

Finally he made up his mind. He sold the little that he had, bought a boat and set off. After a long journey he reached the island of the one-eyed creatures and, indeed, hardly had he stepped ashore when he saw that the people there really had only one eye each.

But of course the one-eyed people noticed that here was a man with two eyes, and a few of them got together and said:

"At last! So this will be our good fortune! Let's catch him and show him in the market-place for a penny a look. We'll soon be rich men!"

No sooner said than done. They seized the two-eyed man and carried him off to the market-place, where they showed him for a penny a look.

And that's the sort of thing that happens to people who sit and wait for unexpected good fortune.

Part Two
ACQUISITION

European powers acquired overseas territories for a variety of reasons, no one of which may yet be said to have been predominant, although in each specific instance of annexation, one motive was uppermost. Often the motivations behind expansion were vague, unspoken, and applied erratically. They included a general desire for personal or national glory, an urge to Christianize native peoples, an assumption that the white race had a mission to uplift a retarded tribe through education, administration, and commerce. On other occasions quite clear reasons could be given at the time, or adduced later, for moving forward: the need for a specific cape, island, river mouth, or harbor in order to further a distinct commercial or strategic interest. For the most part, the decision to intervene in an intertribal war, to send men ashore from a gunboat to pacify a warlike group, or to hold and possess a strategic site was made by a local officer, by a man on the spot who may, or may not, have rightly interpreted instructions sent to him by his superiors in London, Paris, or Berlin, and who may, or may not, have been operating under orders of any kind. In short, personality factors also played a vital role in the events which, on the local scene, propelled the European powers forward, against each other, against indigenous peoples, or merely against unknown landscapes.

It is, nonetheless, customary to speak of at least seven basic thrusts toward imperial expansion: the desire for power, a sense of duty, the wish to promote God's work, racism, commerce and the struggle for markets and suppliers of raw materials and a labor force, national pride, and a romantic wish for adventure. While the "three c's"— commerce, conversion, and competition, together with a fourth, tribal conciliation—may have been uppermost among the forces behind imperialism, none operated to the exclusion of the rest. Spain, Portugal, and the Dutch, later the British and French, and yet later the Germans, Italians, Belgians, Americans, Japanese, and Russians exerted their power over those who had no power for this complex variety of reasons, each of which is illustrated briefly in the documents that follow.

Settlement

The great empires of the eighteenth and early nineteenth centuries were based upon settlement. Settlers would be sent abroad at later dates as well—to Algeria, to the Shiré Highlands, to Alaska—and they were sent to tropical areas on occasion in an earlier period. For the most part, however, the first empire of conscious settlement on a permanent basis was the British, and the plantations, as they were called, were placed in temperate zones: North America, the southwest Pacific, and the southern portion of Africa. There were exceptions, of course—Sierra Leone, on the west coast of Africa and almost entirely black, was a colony of settlement, and portions of the Dutch holdings in the East Indies would become so, as did major areas of the Portuguese empire. But it is to Canada, Australia, and New Zealand in particular that one must look to learn of settlers in action, attempting to create a yeomanry that would provide Britain with a strong right arm overseas.

The following document provides one of several justifications put forward for the swarming of the English, based on "the principle of population," together with an attack on the Corn Laws (those acts which limited trade in grains to the earlier mercantilist pattern), which were to be abolished in 1846, and an analysis of how mother country and colony might benefit from settlement upon the land, even if at the expense of indigenous peoples. This analysis, by Edward Gibbon Wakefield, one of the chief theorists of colonization, is a classic—if ultimately mistaken—effort dating from 1833. Originally appearing in his book of that year, *England and America*, the statement brought together a number of the arguments he had presented four years earlier in his more famous work of epistolary prose. *A Letter from Sydney*, where he had put forward the doctrine of "Sufficient Price" in relation to land. When one remembers that contests over land between settlers and natives were the single greatest cause of conflict between these two groups, one may see the relationship between the arrival of settlers and the "domino theory" of European penetration to the interior of the temperate regions.

From *A Letter from Sydney and Other Writings on Colonization* by Edward Gibbon Wakefield, Everyman's Library Edition (New York: E. P. Dutton & Co., Inc.; London, J. M. Dent & Sons, Ltd., 1929), pp. 109–14, 116–32. Reprinted by permission of the publishers.

The word colony is used to express very different ideas. A conquered nation, amongst whom the victors do not settle, even a mere factory for trade, has commonly been termed a colony; as for example the English factories[1] in India and the actual dominion of the English in

[1] [A factory was a depot, or warehouse, not a place of manufacture.]

that country. Mere stations also for military or trading purposes, such
as Malta and Heligoland, go by the name of colonies. In like manner,
the penal settlements or distant goals of the English are superintended
by their colonial minister, and were called colonies even when their
whole population consisted of prisoners and keepers. Two societies
more different than the people of India ruled by the servants of a
London trading company, and the convicts of New South Wales before
Englishmen not criminals began to settle there, could not well be
imagined. But the difference between the ideas often expressed by
the term colony is matched by the caprice with which that term is
used. The settlements of the Greeks in Sicily and Asia Minor, independent states from the beginning, have always been termed
colonies: the English settlements in America were termed colonies,
though in local matters they governed themselves from the beginning,
so long as England monopolized their foreign trade and managed
their external relations; but from the time when England attempted
to interfere with their domestic government and happily lost both
the monopoly of their foreign trade and the management of their
foreign relations, they have not been reckoned as colonies. According
to the loose way in which this term has been used, it is not dependence that constitutes a colony; nor is it the continual immigration of
people from distant places, since in this respect the United States
surpass all other countries. In order to express the idea of a society,
which continually receives bodies of people from distant places, and
sends out bodies of people to settle permanently in new places, no
distinctive term has yet been used. This, however, is the idea which
will be expressed whenever the term colony is used here; the idea of
a society at once immigrating and emigrating, such as the United
States of America and the English settlements in Canada, South
Africa and Australia.

For the existence of a colony two things are indispensable; first,
waste land, that is, land not yet the property of individuals, but
liable to become so through the intervention of government; and
secondly, the migration of people; the removal of people to settle in
a new place. Further it will be seen at once, that this migration must
be of two kinds; first, the removal of people from an old to a new
country; secondly, the removal of people from a settled part to a
waste part of the colony. Colonization, then, signifies the removal of
people from an old to a new country, and the settlement of people
on the waste land of the new country. As in this there is more to be
done than to be learned, this is an art rather than a science. In every
art, the means to be employed ought to be regulated strictly by the
ends in view. The first point, therefore, in this enquiry is the ends
of colonization.

Two very different societies may have a common interest in coloniza-

tion, though with objects widely different in some respects. The
English, for example, may have a deep interest in removing people
to America for the sake of relief from excessive numbers; while the
Americans, cursed with slavery, might gain incalculably by receiving
numbers of people from England. The ends of colonization, therefore,
may be divided into two classes; those which belong to the old
country, and those which belong to the colony. Each class of objects
will be best ascertained by being examined separately.

It may be questioned whether, in modern times at least, any old
state has founded or extended a colony with any definite object whatever. The states of ancient Greece are supposed by Mr. [James] Mill
to have sent forth bodies of emigrants deliberately with a view to
relief from excessive numbers; and he has shown in a very clear and
forcible manner that the rulers of those states had a strong motive
for seeking that relief in that way, while no such motive was likely
to occur to the rulers of modern Europe. The rulers of modern
Europe, however, have had a motive of affection for colonies. "Sancho
Panza," says Mr. Mill, "had a scheme for deriving advantage from the
government of an island. He would sell the people for slaves and put
the money into his pocket." The Few, in some countries, find in
colonies a thing which is very dear to them; they find, the one part of
them, the precious matter with which to influence; the other, the
precious matter with which *to be* influenced;—the one, the precious
matter with which to make political dependents; the other, the
precious matter with which they are made political dependents; the
one the precious matter by which they augment their power; the other
the precious matter by which they augment their riches. Both portions
of the ruling Few, therefore, find their account in the possession of
colonies. There is not one of the colonies, but what augments the
number of places. There are governorships and judgships and a long
train of *etceteras;* and, above all, there is not one of them but what
requires an additional number of troops and an additional portion
of navy. In every additional portion of army and navy, besides the
glory of the thing, there are generalships and colonelships and captain-
ships, and lieutenantships; and in the equipping and supplying of
additional portions of army and navy, there are always gains which
may be thrown in the way of a friend. All this is enough to account
for a very considerable quantity of affection maintained towards
colonies.

For the affection of the rulers this is enough, but not for that of
the nations. The nations of modern Europe have had a very different
motive of affection for colonies; a sense of the benefits derived from
the discovery of new productions and the creation of new markets.

Those Englishmen, for instance, who during the last century and a half have shouted, "Ships, Colonies and Commerce!" were good political economists. If they did not know scientifically, that all improvements in the productive powers of industry, that industry itself is limited by the extent of the market, still they felt that every new colony, or every enlargement of an old one, increased by so much the means of exchanging the produce of English labour, and by so much increased the wealth of England. Who that produces does not feel, though he may be unable to account for it, the advantage of having some other ready to deal with him for the surplus produce of his labour? A desire for new markets has, indeed, scarcely ever been the deliberate motive for establishing a colony; nor perhaps did any government ever establish a colony deliberately for the sake of patronage. But, colonies having been established, sometimes by the adventurous spirit of individuals, sometimes by religious persecution, the governments and nations of modern Europe had strong motives of affection towards them; the governments, for the sake of patronage; the nations, for the sake of markets. Hence the anxiety of the governments of modern Europe to retain dominion over their colonies, and their attacks upon each other's colonies: hence, too, the Colonial System, as it is called; the system of trading monopolies, which took its rise in a mistaken desire in each nation to monopolize as much as possible of that trade between Europe and her colonies, which would have been more valuable to all the nations if it had been perfectly free. Let us distinguish between the existence and the dominion of a colony; between the existence and the monopoly of a colonial market. "There is no necessity," says Mr. [Jeremy] Bentham, "for governing or possessing any island in order that we may sell merchandize there." But in order to sell merchandize in a colony, it is necessary that the colony should exist. If Mr. Bentham had drawn this distinction, if he had separated the question of dominion from the question of existence, he would not have been led, by dwelling on the evils of colonial monopoly, to undervalue the benefits of colonial trade. His disciple, Mr. Mill, likewise, if he had drawn this distinction, would not have deprecated colonies because they have been made improperly a ground for jobs, monopolies and wars: he might have condemned the wars, monopolies and jobs, of which colonies have been the matter; but perceiving that the real source of those evils was, not the colonies, but the badness of European governments, he would probably have seen also, along with Adam Smith[2] the "natural advantages" which Europe has derived from her colonies, in spite of the tricks which those governments have played with them. The uses and abuses of colonization are very different things. While some philosophers have

[2] [Author of one of the most important analyses of the benefits of free trade, *Wealth of Nations*, published in 1776.]

condemned colonization on account of its abuses, the nations of Europe, even when they promoted the abuses, had, one cannot say a knowledge, but a deep sense of the usefulness. That such "unscientific knowledge," to use terms employed by Bentham, should have been attended with very "unartificial practice," is just what might have been expected.

The objects of an old society in promoting colonization seem to be three: first, the extension of the market for disposing of their own surplus produce; secondly, relief from excessive numbers; thirdly, an enlargement of the field for employing capital. . . . [I]t will be seen presently that these three objects may come under one head; namely, an enlargement of the field for employing capital and labour. But first, each object must be considered separately.

I. THE EXTENSION OF MARKETS

Why does any man ever produce of any thing more than he can himself consume? Solely because he expects that some other man will take from him that portion of the produce of his labour which he does not want, giving him in exchange something which he wants. From the power of exchanging comes every improvement in the application of labour, and every atom of the produce of labour, beyond the rude work and that small produce which supply the wants of savages. It is not because an English washerwoman cannot sit down to breakfast without tea and sugar, that the world has been circumnavigated: but it is because the world has been circumnavigated, that an English washerwoman requires tea and sugar for breakfast. According to the power of exchanging, are the desires of individuals and societies. But every increase of desires, or wants, has a tendency to supply the means of gratification. The savage hunter, enabled to exchange his furs for beads, is stimulated to greater energy and skill. The sole ground on which it is supposed that the blacks of the West Indies will work for wages as soon as they shall be set free, is their love of finery. They will produce sugar, it is said, in order to buy trinkets and fine clothes. And who ever worked hard, when was an improvement made in any useful art, save through the impulse of a passion for some kind of finery; for some gratification, not absolutely necessary, to be obtained by means of exchange? As with individuals, so with nations. In England, the greatest improvements have taken place continually, ever since colonization has continually produced new desires amongst the English, and new markets wherein to purchase the objects of desire. With the growth of sugar and tobacco in America, came the more skilful growth of corn in England. Because, in England, sugar was drank [as rum] and tobacco smoked, corn was raised with less labour, by fewer hands; and more Englishmen existed to eat bread, as well as to drink sugar and smoke tobacco. The removal of Englishmen to America, and their industry in raising new productions not fit for the support of life, led, in England, to more production for the support of life. Because things not necessary had been produced, more necessaries were produced. . . .

But now comes the more interesting case of a society, which, stimulated by the extension of its markets, has cultivated all that part of its territory which is fit for cultivation; a society in which the utmost skill in the application of capital and labour to agriculture is counteracted by the necessity of cultivating inferior land; a society, consequently, in which food is dear, and in which there exist the strongest motives for importing food from other countries by means of manufactures and exchange; a society, in short, which requires new markets in which to purchase the staff of life. This is pre-eminently the case of England. . . .

. . . [F]or such a country as England, a chief end of colonization is to obtain secure markets for the purchase of cheap corn; a steady supply of bread, liable to be increased with an increasing demand.

The trade which the English should conduct for obtaining cheap bread from their colonies might be of two kinds; direct and indirect. Supposing that very cheap corn[3] were raised in Canada, the English might buy such corn with the manufactured goods of Leeds, Manchester and Birmingham; this would be a direct trade. But it might very well happen that the Canadians should be able to raise, not more corn than the English should be able to buy, but more than they should be able to buy *with manufactured goods*. In other words, the demand of the Canadians for English goods might be much less than the demand of the English for Canadian corn. But the Canadians would require many things, besides English goods, which are not producible in Canada: they would require tea and silver, for instance. The English, then, might first buy tea and silver of the Chinese with manufactured goods, and then buy corn of the Canadians with tea and silver. But the demand, again, of the Chinese for English goods might not be sufficient to supply in this way the demand of the English for Canadian corn. For one thing, however, the demand of the Chinese is very urgent and would be without limit; for food in every shape; for the means of life. Here, then, is the groundwork of the most extensive commerce that ever existed in the world. Supposing that cheap food were raised in the English colonies of Australia, which, though far from England, are near to China, the English might buy such food with manufactured goods; with that food buy tea and silver of the Chinese; and with that tea and silver, buy cheap

[3] [That is, all forms of grain.]

corn of the Canadians. In this case, combination of capital and labour for division of employments amongst four different nations, would be of the greatest service to all of them: to the Australian colonists, the Chinese, the Canadian colonists, and the English. A great number of cases like this might be reasonably supposed. . . .

But it may be said, a country like England, having no corn laws, might obtain all these benefits without colonies. "The possession of colonies," Sir Henry Parnell[4] would say, "affords no advantages which could not be obtained by commercial intercourse with independent states." Here again the question of dominion is mixed up with the question of existence. Independent states! which are the independent states that could produce very cheap corn for the English market? The United States: truly; but the United States are as much colonies as were the never dependent colonies of Greece. Canada, on the other hand, being dependent, is neither more nor less fit than the United States to produce cheap corn for the English market. Let us banish altogether, for the present, the idea of monopoly or dominion. Of him who has done this, I would ask, What country, in which land is cheap, is most fit, on other accounts, to provide the English with cheap corn? Not Poland; because there property is insecure, industry unskilful and the people barbarous; not Buenos Ayres, where land is cheaper than in any other country, being obtainable in unlimited quantities for nothing, of the richest quality, already cleared and drained by nature; . . . not Ceylon; because, though that country be improperly called an English colony, its inhabitants are not anxious to obtain English goods: none of these, but the United States, Canada and the English settlements in South Africa and Australia; because, in all of those countries, corn might be raised on cheap land, with English skill, by people anxious to buy English goods. . . .

II. RELIEF FROM EXCESSIVE NUMBERS

In modern times, no old country has ever obtained relief from excessive numbers by means of colonization. In no case, has the number of emigrants been sufficient to diminish, even for a year, the ruinous competition of labourers for employment; much less to produce any lasting improvement in the condition of the bulk of the people. More than once, however, this has been the object, or has been called the object, of an old state in promoting colonization. Twice since their late war with the French, the English have sent out bodies of people to colonies under the rule of the English government,

[4] [A Radical member of Parliament who, in his book *On Financial Reform*, published in 1830, called for a reduction in colonies, retaining only those which supported their own defense.]

for the declared purpose of checking pauperism at home: first to the Dutch colony of South Africa, and next to the English colony of Upper Canada.[5] On neither of these occasions was the object attained even in the slightest degree. Both these attempts were called experiments. . . . To call experiments measures so futile, so obviously inadequate to the end in view, is an abuse of language; and one calculated to be mischievous; since, if these childish attempts had really been experiments, the signal failure of them would have been a fact tending to establish, that colonization with a view to relief from excessive numbers must necessarily fail of its object.

Two classes of men in England, classes of the most opposite turn of mind, have decided against colonization with this view; and on grounds equally unreasonable: first, those unreasoning men who would determine questions in political economy by quoting scripture; secondly, men who possess in a high degree the faculty of reason, but who, having made a religion for themselves, are often under the influence of a kind of bigotry; I mean those political economists who worship capital. Speak of emigration to one of the former class, and he will exclaim, "Dwell in the land and verily ye shall be fed"; to one of the latter, and he will say,—The question deserves profound regard; but as employment for labour is in proportion to capital, as emigration would cost money and diminish capital, therefore it would diminish employment for labour and do more harm than good.

Whether right or wrong in their dislike of emigration, those who swear by David, and those who worship capital, are equally contradicted by facts. The people do dwell in the land, but verily they are not fed. Though no labour be employed save by capital, still millions upon millions of capital are accumulated, not to employ domestic labour, but, for want of employment *for capital,* either to lie idle, or to be wasted in distant and ruinous speculations. The quotation from scripture may be disposed of by another: "Increase and multiply, and *replenish the earth, and subdue it.*" But those who object to emigration on the score of its expense deserve, on account of their reputation and authority, that their argument should be carefully examined.

The argument is stated as follows, by Mr. Mill:

It has been often enough, and clearly enough explained, that it is capital which gives employment to labour: we may, therefore, take it as a postulate. A certain quantity of capital, then, is necessary to give employment to the population, which any removal for the sake of colonization may leave behind. But *if,* to afford the expense of that removal, so much is taken from the capital of the country that the remainder is not sufficient for the employment of the remaining population, there is, in that case, a redundancy of population, and all the evils which it brings. For the well-being of the remaining population, a certain quantity of food is required, and a certain quantity of all those other things which minister to human happiness. But to raise this quantity of other things, a certain quantity of capital is indispensably necessary. *If* that quantity of capital is not supplied, the food and other things cannot be obtained.

. . . Now upon what rests this assumption? It rests upon two other assumptions, one of which is true, the other false; first, that no labour is employed save by capital; secondly, that all capital employs labour. If it were true that every increase of capital necessarily gave employment to more labour; if it were true . . . that "there is plainly only one way of effectually improving the condition of the great majority of the community or of the labouring class, and that is *by increasing the ratio of capital to population,*" then it might be assumed that colonization would, on account of its expense, do more harm than good. But it is not true that all capital employs labour. To say so, is to say that which a thousand facts prove to be untrue. Capital frequently increases without providing any more employment for labour. . . . It follows, that capital, for which there is no employment at home, might be spent on emigration without diminishing employment for labour to the slightest extent. I use the word *spent* instead of *invested,* in order to save the trouble of explaining at length, that if capital so employed were utterly lost, that loss of capital need not diminish employment for labour. No one pretends that employment for English labour was diminished, to the extent of a single pair of hands, by the loans which the English lately made to the republics, so called, of South America . . . ; or by the late waste of English capital in pretending to work mines in South America, or in glutting distant markets with English goods sold for less than the cost of production; or by the waste of English capital in founding the Swan River settlement [in Western Australia]. Still less has employment for English labour been diminished by late investments of English capital, in foreign countries, which yield some return: such as loans to the emperors of Austria and Russia, to the kings of Prussia, Naples, the Low Countries and France; purchases lately made in the securities of foreign governments, amounting at one time in the French funds alone to near £40,000,000; investments of English capital in the iron and cotton works of France, the Low Countries and Germany; and finally, loans to the North American States. If all the capital removed from England in all these ways during the last seventeen years, amounting to some hundreds of millions, had been lost in conducting emigration, employment for labour in England would not have been less than it is at present.

*   *   *

Supposing that, whether by means of English capital about, at all events, to fly off to foreign countries, or by means of a fund raised in the colonies, such an amount of labour should emigrate from England as considerably to diminish the proportion which, in England, labour bears to employment, then would the wages of labour be higher, then would the state of the bulk of the people be improved, then would relief be obtained from excessive numbers. This great end of colonization has never been so much as seriously contemplated by the ruling class in England. . . . Late events have produced some change of feeling on this subject; and coming events, probably, will soon produce a greater change. . . . The new ruling class of England, those whom late events have made the great men of England, are placed in a situation which may render excess of numbers highly disagreeable to them. They may be glad to pay high wages for the security of their property; to prevent the devastation of England through commotions arising from discontent in the bulk of the people. Even before the late change[6] while the fears of the great men were urging them to bring about that change, while fires were blazing and mobs exacting higher wages in the south of England, a dread of the political evils likely to come from excessive numbers, induced the English Government to form a Board of Emigration, with the avowed purpose of improving the condition of the labouring class, by removing some of them to the colonies. A more foolish, or rather futile, effort by great men to remove what they felt as disagreeable, was perhaps never made; but the effort, feeble and puerile though it were, tends to point out that for a country situated like England, in which the ruling and the subject orders are no longer separated by a middle class, and in which the subject order, composing the bulk of the people, are in a state of gloomy discontent arising from excessive numbers; that for such a country, one chief end of colonization is to prevent tumults, to keep the peace, to maintain order, to uphold confidence in the security of property, to hinder interruptions of the regular course of industry and trade, to avert the terrible evils which, in a country like England, could not but follow any serious political convulsion.

For England, another end of colonization, by means of relief from excessive numbers, would be relief from that portion of the poor's-rate which maintains workmen in total or partial idleness; an object in which the ruling order have an obvious interest.

For England again, a very useful end of colonization would be to turn the tide of Irish emigration from England to her colonies; not to mention that the owners of land in Ireland, most of them being foreigners by religion, might thus be taken out of the dilemma in which they are now placed: that of a choice between legally giving up

[6] [The reform bill of 1832.]

a great part of their rental to the hungry people, and yielding to the people's violence the land which was taken by violence from their fathers.

Finally, comprised in relief from excessive numbers is the relief to many classes, not called labourers or capitalists, from that excessive competition for employment which renders them uneasy and dissatisfied. Of the 125,000 persons who quitted England last year to settle in colonies, not a few were professional men: surgeons, clergymen, lawyers, architects, engineers, surveyors, teachers and clerks: some few of them were governesses. . . .

III. Enlargement of the Field for Employing Capital

This end of colonization is distinct from that enlargement of the field for employing capital, which would come by the creation of extensive markets for the purchase of cheap corn with the produce of domestic industry. It may be best explained by reference to some facts. Since England began to colonize, how many Englishmen have quitted their country with small fortunes, and returned with large ones, made by means of high profits in the colonies! In the West India islands alone, millions upon millions of English capital have been employed with very great profit; millions upon millions, which, we may be sure, would not have been removed to the West Indies, if they could have been invested at home with equal profit. An existing London Company has more than doubled its capital in a few years, besides paying a handsome dividend to the shareholders, by the purchase and sale of waste land in Upper Canada. . . . Examples without end might be adduced of profitable investments made by the people of old states in new colonies; and made, too, without any permanent abstraction of capital from the old country. . . . To say that because English capital has been wasted in colonies, no more capital ought to be invested in that way, would be like saying, that because Waterloo bridge yields no profit to those who built it, no more bridges ought to be built. . . .

*   *   *

I have attempted to prove elsewhere, that want of free labour is the cause of slavery in America; not the dearness of labour, but the want of free labour at any price. Why do the settlers in New South Wales, having capital, dread above all things that the English Government should cease to pour into that colony a stream of population utterly depraved and irreclaimable? The criminal code of England is more bloody than that of any other country which has a code of laws; but in

New South Wales, the proportion of public executions to public executions in England is, I believe, allowing for the difference of numbers, in the ratio of 325 to 1. This is partly accounted for when we reflect, that, of the convicts sent to New South Wales, nine out of ten are men, brought to that pass, most of them, by the violence of their passions; nine men to one woman; men accustomed to unbridled indulgence and reckless of all social ties. The result need not be described. Nor is it difficult to account for the attachment of the English Government to this system of Reformation. If English convicts were punished by imprisonment at home, though the English aristocracy would have, to bestow upon their dependants, more places such as that of jailer or turnkey, they would miss the disposal of a number of places such as gentlemen will accept. The governor of New South Wales is a jailer; but, being called Your Excellency, and paid accordingly, he is thankful for his place; as thankful as anyone ever is for a place which he has obtained by electioneering services. But how are we to account for the attachment of the richer colonists to this horrid system of transportation? By their want of free labour; by their anxiety to keep that slave labour, without which each of them could use no more capital than his own hands could employ. They say, and with perfect truth, that if the supply of convicts were stopped the colony would be ruined. Assuredly the colony would be ruined, unless the richer settlers should find the means of obtaining either free labour, or that kind of slave labour which they have in America.

But even with the convict system, there is a deficiency of labour. In Van Diemen's Land, it is common to see one, two or three, thousand sheep all in one flock, the old and the young, the strong and the weak, all mixed together. While feeding, the strongest of a flock, so mixed, always take the van, the weakest always bringing up the rear. Thus a great number of the lambs or weaker sheep are starved to death; and, of course, the profits of the owner of the flock are by so much diminished. Why is this loss incurred? for want of more shepherds; of more labour. If there were in Van Diemen's Land shepherds enough to manage all the flocks in the best way, the increase of produce would give higher wages to the greater number of labourers, besides augmenting the profits of the flock owners. The soil and climate of New South Wales appear admirably suited to the growth of tobacco, olive oil, silk, and wine. A London company has spent near £300,000 with the intention, declared by its prospectus, of growing all these things in New South Wales. Why has it not grown any of these things? Because for the growth of any of these things constant and combined labour is required; an element of production wanting in New South Wales. Convict labour, though constant when compared with such labour as is got by the occasional immigration of free workmen, is very inconstant when compared with the labour of negro slaves. The convict works only so long as his term of punishment lasts, and for one master only so long as the governor pleases, or the secretary of the governor, or the superintendent of convicts, or some members of the colonial council; any one of whom may suddenly, and without rhyme or reason, deprive a settler of his convict servants. While slave labour may be combined in quantities proportioned to the capitalist's means of buying slaves, convict labour can never be combined in large quantities; because, as the government bestows this labour, if any one settler should obtain more than his due share of convicts, all the others would complain of gross partiality; and because the proportion of convicts to settlers is so small, that without gross partiality no one settler can have more than a few pairs of convict hands. Favoured settlers, those who find favour with the governor and his officers, do often obtain more than a fair share of convicts; but, as the favour of governors is uncertain, no motive is furnished, even in these cases of gross partiality, for the commencement of works which require the constant employment of many hands, at the same time, in the same place, and for a period of consecutive years. . . .

In Canada, as in the United States, there is a want of free labour for works which require the combination of many hands and divison of employments. The canals which the English government has lately formed in Canada could not have been finished, or perhaps begun, without a supply of labour from Ireland. The great Lake Erie canal, a work of which the public advantage, and the profit to the undertakers, was made manifest upon paper long before the work was begun, could not perhaps have been begun, most certainly could not have been finished, without a great supply of Irish labour. . . . If the means by which the United States, Canada and New South Wales, obtain labour, should be taken away, no others being supplied, then must those colonies soon fall into the miserable state of other colonies which have never had any means of obtaining labour. In a word, from whatever point of view we look at this subject, it appears that the great want of colonies is Labour, the original purchase-money of all things.

The elements of colonization, it is quite obvious, are waste land and the removal of people. If there were no waste land, no people would remove; if no people would remove, waste land must remain in a desert state. Waste land is cultivated by the removal of people, and people are removed by means of the motive to removal furnished by the existence of waste land. Capital for the removal of people, and for the settlement of people on waste land, being included in the ideas of removal and settlement, the means of colonization, it follows inevitably, will resolve themselves into the disposal of waste land for the removal of people. . . .

The disposal of waste land for the removal of people might be considered in two different points of view: first, as that element of colonization is liable to be used by an old state; and secondly, as it is liable to be used by a colony. Both these ways of examining the subject would lead to the same conclusion. For instance, we should determine the best mode of treating waste land, either by ascertaining how the United States might best dispose of waste land for the removal of people, or how the English, with the same object, might best dispose of waste land in Canada or Australia. But considering that the removal of people is a secondary means of colonization, depending on the disposal of waste land; seeing that it is waste land which draws people from the settled to the waste parts of the colony, and so makes room for the arrival of people from an old country, and that this prime mover, or point of attraction, exists in the colony, it will be found much more convenient to look at the means of colonization from a colonial position. If this course had been pursued before, the English would not have been as ignorant as they are of the political economy of new countries. Their economists, in treating of colonies, have worked with no other tools than those which they were accustomed to use in explaining the phenomena of an old country; have reasoned from principles, that were true in the old country, to facts that never existed in the colony. They remind one of an Englishman who, having been used to the luxury of music, carried a grand upright piano to the Swan River, and then, finding no body to make a cupboard for him, was fain to gut the musical instrument and use it for holding his crockery; or of that English colonial minister, who, knowing that in Europe the seas are salt, sent waterbutts from England for the use of the English fleet on a freshwater sea in America. By looking at this subject from a colonial position, we shall proceed from facts to conclusions. . . .

Capitalism and Commerce

Unquestionably one of the great "engines" of expansion was capitalism. But what kind of capitalism, at what stage, under what conditions, and for what reasons? A classic, and much-debated, answer was given to these questions by V. I. Lenin in 1916. *Imperialism: The Highest Stage of Capitalism*, penned in Zurich and drawing upon another famous analysis, J. A. Hobson's *Imperialism*, published in London in 1902, was both an attempt to account for imperialism in the evolution and degeneration of capitalism, and to fire a number of heavy salvoes at those Marxists and petit bourgeois revisionists with whom Lenin disagreed. In the statement that follows one gains, therefore, insights not only into the Leninist position, but into those of Karl Kautsky and others. One might wish to read the selection from Frantz Fanon, in the final portion of this book, together with that by Lenin, as both provide a framework for understanding the violence which was sometimes the necessary reply to imperialism.

From *Imperialism: The Highest Stage of Capitalism*, third edition, by V. I. Lenin (New York: International Publishers, 1939), pp. 88–93, 96–98. Reprinted by permission of the publisher.

We must now try to sum up and put together what [we have] said on the subject of imperialism. Imperialism emerged as the development and direct continuation of the fundamental attributes of capitalism in general. But capitalism only became capitalist imperialism at a definite and very high stage of its development, when certain of its fundamental attributes began to be transformed into their opposites, when the features of a period of transition from capitalism to a higher social and economic system began to take shape and reveal themselves all along the line. Economically, the main thing in this process is the substitution of capitalist monopolies for capitalist free competition. Free competition is the fundamental attribute of capitalism, and of commodity production generally. Monopoly is exactly the opposite of free competition; but we have seen the latter being transformed into monopoly before our very eyes, creating large-scale industry and eliminating small industry, replacing large-scale industry by still larger-scale industry, finally leading to such a concentration of production and capital that monopoly has been and is the result: cartels, syndicates and trusts, and merging with them, the capital of a dozen or so banks manipulating thousands of millions. At the same time monopoly, which has grown out of free competition, does not abolish the latter, but exists over it and alongside of it, and thereby gives rise to a number of very acute, intense antagonisms, friction and conflicts. Monopoly is the transition from capitalism to a higher system.

If it were necessary to give the briefest possible definition of imperialism we should have to say that imperialism is the monopoly stage of capitalism. Such a definition would include what is most important, for, on the one hand, finance capital is the bank capital of a few big monopolist banks, merged with the capital of the monopolist combines of manufacturers; and, on the other hand, the division of the world is the transition from a colonial policy which has extended without hindrance to territories unoccupied by any capitalist power, to a colonial policy of monopolistic possession of the territory of the world which has been completely divided up.

But very brief definitions, although convenient, for they sum up the main points, are nevertheless inadequate, because very important features of the phenomenon that has to be defined have to be especially deduced. And so, without forgetting the conditional and relative value of all definitions, which can never include all the concatenations of a phenomenon in its complete development, we must give a definition of imperialism that will embrace the following five essential features:

1) The concentration of production and capital developed to such a high stage that it created monopolies which play a decisive role in economic life.

2) The merging of bank capital with industrial capital, and the creation, on the basis of this "finance capital," of a "financial oligarchy."

3) The export of capital, which has become extremely important, as distinguished from the export of commodities.

4) The formation of international capitalist monopolies which share the world among themselves.

5) The territorial division of the whole world among the greatest capitalist powers is completed.

Imperialism is capitalism in that stage of development in which the dominance of monopolies and finance capital has established itself; in which the export of capital has acquired pronounced importance; in which the division of the world among the international trusts has begun; in which the division of all territories of the globe among the great capitalist powers has been completed. . . .

. . . The point to be noted just now is that imperialism, as interpreted above, undoubtedly represents a special stage in the development of capitalism. In order to enable the reader to obtain as well grounded an idea of imperialism as possible, we deliberately quoted largely from *bourgeois* economists who are obliged to admit the particularly incontrovertible facts regarding modern capitalist economy. . . . Needless to say, all boundaries in nature and in society are conditional and changeable, and consequently, it would be absurd to discuss the exact year or the decade in which imperialism "definitely" became established.

In this matter of defining imperialism, however, we have to enter into controversy, primarily, with K. Kautsky, the principal Marxian theoretician of the epoch of the so-called Second International—that is, of the twenty-five years between 1889 and 1914.

Kautsky, in 1915 and even in November 1914, very emphatically attacked the fundamental ideas expressed in our definition of imperialism. Kautsky said that imperialism must not be regarded as a "phase" or stage of economy, but as a policy; a definite policy "preferred" by finance capital; that imperialism cannot be "identified" with "contemporary capitalism"; that if imperialism is to be understood to mean "all the phenomena of contemporary capitalism"—cartels, protection, the domination of the financiers and colonial policy—then the question as to whether imperialism is necessary to capitalism becomes reduced to the "flattest tautology"; because, in that case, "imperialism is naturally a vital necessity for capitalism," and so on. The best way to present Kautsky's ideas is to quote his own definition of imperialism, which is diametrically opposed to the substance of the ideas which we have set forth (for the objections coming from the camp of the German Marxists, who have been advocating such ideas for many years already, have been long known to Kautsky as the objections of a definite trend in Marxism).

Kautsky's definition is as follows:

> Imperialism is a product of highly developed industrial capitalism. It consists in the striving of every industrial capitalist nation to bring under its control and to annex increasingly big *agrarian* (Kautsky's italics) regions irrespective of what nations inhabit those regions.

This definition is utterly worthless because it one-sidedly, *i.e.*, arbitrarily, brings out the national question alone (although this is extremely important in itself as well as in its relation to imperialism), it arbitrarily and *inaccurately* relates this question *only* to industrial capital in the countries which annex other nations, and in an equally arbitrary and inaccurate manner brings out the annexation of agrarian regions.

Imperialism is a striving for annexations—this is what the *political* part of Kautsky's definition amounts to. It is correct, but very incomplete, for politically, imperialism is, in general, a striving towards violence and reaction. For the moment, however, we are interested in the *economic* aspect of the question, which Kautsky *himself* introduced into *his* definition. The inaccuracy of Kautsky's definition is strikingly obvious. The characteristic feature of imperialism is *not* industrial capital, *but* finance capital. It is not an accident that in France it was precisely the extraordinarily rapid development of *finance* capital, and the weakening of industrial capital, that, from 1880 onwards, gave rise to the extreme extension of annexationist (colonial) policy. The characteristic feature of imperialism is precisely that it strives to annex *not only* agricultural regions, but even highly industrialised regions (German appetite for Belgium; French appetite for Lorraine), because 1) the fact that the world is already divided up obliges those contemplating a *new* division to reach out for *any kind* of territory, and 2) because an essential feature of imperialism is the rivalry between a number of great powers in the striving for hegemony, *i.e.*, for the conquest of territory, not so much directly for themselves as to weaken the adversary and undermine *his* hegemony. (Belgium is chiefly necessary to Germany as a base for operations against England; England needs Bagdad as a base for operations against Germany, etc.)

Kautsky refers especially—and repeatedly—to English writers who, he alleges, have given a purely political meaning to the word "imperialism" in the sense that Kautsky understands it. We take up the work by the Englishman Hobson, *Imperialism,* which appeared in 1902, and therein we read:

> The new imperialism differs from the older, first, in substituting for the ambition of a single growing empire the theory and the practice of competing empires, each motivated by similar lusts of political aggrandisement and commercial gain; secondly, in the dominance of financial or investing over mercantile interests.

We see, therefore, that Kautsky is absolutely wrong in referring to English writers generally (unless he meant the vulgar English imperialist writers, or the avowed apologists for imperialism). We see that Kautsky, while claiming that he continues to defend Marxism, as a matter of fact takes a step backward compared with the *social-liberal* Hobson, who *more correctly* takes into account two "historically concrete" (Kautsky's definition is a mockery of historical concreteness) features of modern imperialism: 1) the competition between *several* imperialisms, and 2) the predominance of the financier over the merchant. If it were chiefly a question of the annexation of agrarian countries by industrial countries, the role of the merchant would be predominant.

Kautsky's definition is not only wrong and un-Marxian. It serves as a basis for a whole system of views which run counter to Marxian theory and Marxian practice all along the line. . . . The argument about words which Kautsky raises as to whether the modern stage of capitalism should be called "imperialism" or "the stage of finance capital" is of no importance. Call it what you will, it matters little. The fact of the matter is that Kautsky detaches the politics of imperialism from its economics, speaks of annexations as being a policy "preferred" by finance capital, and opposes to it another bourgeois policy which, hc alleges, is possible on this very basis of finance capital. According to his argument, monopolies in economics are compatible with non-monopolistic, non-violent, non-annexationist methods in politics. According to his argument, the territorial division of the world, which was completed precisely during the period of finance capital, and which constitutes the basis of the present peculiar forms of rivalry between the biggest capitalist states, is compatible with a non-imperialist policy. The result is a slurring-over and a blunting of the most profound contradictions of the latent stage of capitalism, instead of an exposure of their depth; the result is bourgeois reformism instead of Marxism. . . .

There are two areas where capitalism is not strongly developed: Russia and Eastern Asia. In the former, the density of population is very low, in the latter it is very high; in the former political concentration is very high, in the latter it does not exist. The partition of China is only beginning, and the struggle between Japan, U.S.A., etc., in connection therewith is continually gaining in intensity.

Compare this reality, the vast diversity of economic and political conditions, the extreme disparity in the rate of development of the various countries, etc., and the violent struggles of the imperialist states, with Kautsky's silly little fable about "peaceful" ultra-imperialism. . . . Is not American and other finance capital, which divided the whole world peacefully, with Germany's participation, for example, in the international rail syndicate, or in the international mercantile shipping trust, now engaged in *redividing* the world on the basis of a new relation of forces, which has been changed by methods *by no means* peaceful?

Finance capital and the trusts are increasing instead of diminishing the differences in the rate of development of the various parts of world economy. When the relation of forces is changed, how else, *under capitalism,* can the solution of contradictions be found, except by resorting to *violence?* Railway statistics provide remarkably exact data on the different rates of development of capitalism and finance capital in world economy. In the last decades of imperialist development, the total length of railways has changed as [table, opposite, indicates].

Thus, the development of railways has been more rapid in the colonies and in the independent (and semi-dependent) states of Asia and America. Here, as we know, the finance capital of the four or five biggest capitalist states reigns undisputed. Two hundred thousand kilometres of new railways in the colonies and in the other countries of Asia and America represent more than 40,000,000,000 marks in

RAILWAYS (*thousand kilometres*)

	1890	1913	Increase
Europe	224	346	122
U.S.A.	268	411	143
Colonies (total)	82 ⎱	210 ⎱	128 ⎱
Independent and semi-dependent states of Asia and America	43 ⎰ 125	137 ⎰ 347	94 ⎰ 222
Total	617	1,104	

capital, newly invested on particularly advantageous terms, with special guarantees of a good return and with profitable orders for steel works, etc., etc.

Capitalism is growing with the greatest rapidity in the colonies and in overseas countries. Among the latter, *new* imperialist powers are emerging (*e.g.,* Japan). The struggle of world imperialism is becoming more acute. The tribute levied by finance capital on the most profitable colonial and overseas enterprises is increasing. In sharing out this "booty," an exceptionally large part goes to countries which, as far as the development of productive forces is concerned, do not always stand at the top of the list. In the case of the biggest countries, considered with their colonies, the total length of railways was as follows (in thousands of kilometres):

	1890	1913	Increase
U.S.A.	268	413	145
British Empire	107	208	101
Russia	32	78	46
Germany	43	68	25
France	41	63	22
Total	491	830	339

Thus, about 80 per cent of the total existing railways are concentrated in the hands of the five Great Powers. But the concentration of the *ownership* of these railways, of finance capital, is much greater still: French and English millionaires, for example, own an enormous amount of stocks and bonds in American, Russian and other railways.

Thanks to her colonies, Great Britain has increased the length of "her" railways by 100,000 kilometres, four times as much as Germany. And yet, it is well known that the development of productive forces in Germany, and especially the development of the coal and iron industries, has been much more rapid during this period than in England—not to mention France and Russia. In 1892, Germany produced 4,900,000 tons of pig iron and Great Britain produced 6,800,000 tons; in 1912, Germany produced 17,600,000 tons and Great Britain 9,000,000 tons. Germany, therefore, had an overwhelming superiority over England in this respect. We ask, is there *under capitalism* any means of removing the disparity between the development of productive forces and the accumulation of capital on the one side, and the division of colonies and "spheres of influence" for finance capital on the other side—other than by resorting to war?

Power and Pride

Count von Bülow, who in 1897 became Prince Bismarck's Foreign Secretary, recognized the sense of pride in himself, when he declared that, "Where I have planted my foot, there shall no one else be permitted to place his." One year after, Balliol-educated Hilaire Belloc would remind himself of the technological reality that lay behind power:

> I never shall forget the way
> That Blood upon this awful day
> Preserved us all from death.
> He stood upon a little mound,
> Cast his lethargic eyes around,
> And said beneath his breath:
> "Whatever happens we have got
> The Maxim gun, and they have not."

Maxim, Bofors, Colt, or Remington, the distich of William Blood was to the point: he who held the top of the hill, who had the best weaponry, the largest battalions, the swiftest navy held power (and thus pride) in his hands.

But need this power, and the lust for more of it, be a monopoly of the capitalists, and need it—as Lenin argued—be the hallmark of their decay? Joseph A. Schumpeter, a Moravian-born economist who was a professor of economics in Germany, from which he came to the United States in 1932, thought not. In an essay, "Zur Soziologie der Imperialismus," which was first published in 1919—although not in English until 1951—he argued that capitalist societies were not inherently imperialistic and offered a sociological and psychological theory to account for the imperialism they nonetheless unquestionably had shown.

From *Imperialism and Social Classes* by Joseph A. Schumpeter, trans. Heinz Norden, ed. Paul M. Sweezy (New York: Augustus M. Kelley, 1951), pp. 64–76, 96–98. Copyright, 1951, by Elizabeth B. Schumpeter. Reprinted by permission of the President and Fellows of Harvard College.

Our analysis of the historical evidence has shown, first, the unquestionable fact that "objectless" tendencies toward forcible expansion, without definite, utilitarian limits—that is, non-rational and irrational, purely instinctual inclinations toward war and conquest—play a very large role in the history of mankind. It may sound paradoxical, but numberless wars—perhaps the majority of all wars—have been waged without adequate "reason"—not so much from the moral viewpoint as from that of reasoned and reasonable interest. . . .

Our analysis, in the second place, provides an explanation for this drive to action, this will to war—a theory by no means exhausted by mere references to an "urge" or an "instinct." The explanation lies, instead, in the vital needs of situations that molded peoples and classes into warriors—if they wanted to avoid extinction—and in the fact that psychological dispositions and social structures acquired in the dim past in such situations, once firmly established, tend to maintain themselves and to continue in effect long after they have lost their meaning and their life-preserving function. Our analysis, in the third place, has shown the existence of subsidiary factors that facilitate the survival of such dispositions and structures—factors that may be divided into two groups. The orientation toward war is mainly fostered by the domestic interests of ruling classes, but also by the influence of all those who stand to gain individually from a war policy, whether economically or socially. Both groups of factors are generally overgrown by elements of an altogether different character, not only in terms of political phraseology, but also of psychological motivation. Imperialisms differ greatly in detail, but they all have at least these traits in common, turning them into a single phenomenon in the field of sociology. . . .

Imperialism thus is atavistic in character. It falls into that large group of surviving features from earlier ages that play such an important part in every concrete social situation. In other words, it is an element that stems from the living conditions, not of the present, but of the past—or, put in terms of the economic interpretation of history, from past rather than present relations of production. It is an atavism in the social structure, in individual, psychological habits of emotional reaction. Since the vital needs that created it have passed away for good, it too must gradually disappear, even though every warlike involvement, no matter how non-imperialist in character, tends to revive it. It tends to disappear as a structural element because the structure that brought it to the fore goes into a decline, giving way, in the course of social development, to other structures that have no room for it and eliminate the power factors that supported it. It tends to disappear as an element of habitual emotional reaction, because of the progressive rationalization of life and mind, a process in which old functional needs are absorbed by new tasks, in which heretofore military energies are functionally modified. . . .

It is from absolute autocracy that the present age has taken over what imperialist tendencies it displays. And the imperialism of absolute autocracy flourished before the Industrial Revolution that created the modern world, or rather, before the consequences of that revolution began to be felt in all their aspects. These two statements are primarily meant in a historical sense, and as such they are no more than self-evident. We shall nevertheless try, within the framework of our theory, to define the significance of capitalism for our phenomenon and to examine the relationship between present-day imperialist tendencies and the autocratic imperialism of the eighteenth century.

The floodtide that burst the dams in the Industrial Revolution had its sources, of course, back in the Middle Ages. But capitalism began to shape society and impress its stamp on every page of social history only with the second half of the eighteenth century. Before that time there had been only islands of capitalist economy imbedded in an ocean of village and urban economy. True, certain political influences emanated from these islands, but they were able to assert themselves only indirectly. Not until the process we term the Industrial Revolution did the working masses, led by the entrepreneur, overcome the bonds of older life-forms—the environment of peasantry, guild, and aristocracy. The causal connection was this: a transformation in the basic economic factors (which need not detain us here) created the objective opportunity for the production of commodities, for large-scale industry, working for a market of customers whose individual identities were unknown, operating solely with a view to maximum financial profit. It was this opportunity that created an economically oriented leadership—personalities whose field of achievement was the organization of such commodity production in the form of capitalist enterprise. Successful enterprises in large numbers represented something new in the economic and social sense. They fought for and won freedom of action. They compelled state policy to adapt itself to their needs. More and more they attracted the most vigorous leaders from other spheres, as well as the manpower of those spheres, causing them and the social strata they represented to languish. Capitalist entrepreneurs fought the former ruling circles for a share in state control, for leadership in the state. The very fact of their success, their position, their resources, their power, raised them in the political and social scale. Their mode of life, their cast of mind became increasingly important elements on the social scene. Their actions, desires, needs, and beliefs emerged more and more sharply within the total picture of the social community. In a historical sense, this applied primarily to the industrial and financial leaders of the movement—the bourgeoisie. But soon it applied also to the working masses which this movement created and placed in an altogether new class situation. This situation was governed by new forms of the working day, of family life, of interests—and these, in turn, corresponded to new orientations toward the social structure as a whole. More and more, in the course of the nineteenth century, the typical modern worker came to determine the over-all aspect of society; for competitive capitalism, by its inherent logic, kept on raising the demand for labor and thus the economic level and social power of the workers, until this class too was able to assert itself in a political sense. The working class and its mode of life provided the type from which the intellectual developed. Capitalism did not create the intellectuals—the "new middle class." But in earlier times only the legal scholar, the cleric, and the physician had formed a special intellectual class, and even they had enjoyed but little scope for playing an independent role. Such opportunities were provided only by capitalist society, which created the industrial and financial bureaucrat, the journalist, and so on, and which opened up new vistas to the jurist and physician. The "professional" of capitalist society arose as a class type. Finally, as a class type, the rentier, the beneficiary of industrial loan capital, is also a creature of capitalism. All these types are shaped by the capitalist mode of production, and they tend for this reason to bring other types—even the peasant—into conformity with themselves.

These new types were now cast adrift from the fixed order of earlier times, from the environment that had shackled and protected people for centuries, from the old associations of village, manor house, clan fellowship, often even from families in the broader sense. They were severed from the things that had been constant year after year, from cradle to grave—tools, homes, the countryside, especially the soil. They were on their own, enmeshed in the pitiless logic of gainful employment, mere drops in the vast ocean of industrial life, exposed to the inexorable pressures of competition. They were freed from the control of ancient patterns of thought, of the grip of institutions and organs that taught and represented these outlooks in village, manor, and guild. They were removed from the old world, engaged in building a new one for themselves—a specialized, mechanized world. Thus they were all inevitably democratized, individualized, and rationalized. They were democratized, because the picture of time-honored power and privilege gave way to one of continual change, set in motion by industrial life. They were individualized, because subjective opportunities to shape their lives took the place of immutable objective factors. They were rationalized, because the instability of economic position made their survival hinge on continual, deliberately rationalistic decisions—a dependence that emerged with great sharpness. Trained to economic rationalism, these people left no sphere of life unrationalized, questioning everything about themselves, the social structure, the state, the ruling class. The marks of this process are engraved on every aspect of modern culture. It is this process that explains the basic features of that culture.

These are things that are well known today, recognized in their full significance—indeed, often exaggerated. Their application to our subject is plain. Everything that is purely instinctual, everything insofar as it is purely instinctual, is driven into the background by this development. It creates a social and psychological atmosphere in keeping with modern economic forms, where traditional habits, merely because they were traditional, could no more survive than obsolete economic forms. Just as the latter can survive only if they are continually "adapted," so instinctual tendencies can survive only when the conditions that gave rise to them continue to apply, or when the "instinct" in question derives a new purpose from new conditions. The "instinct" that is *only* "instinct," that has lost its purpose, languishes relatively quickly in the capitalist world, just as does an inefficient economic practice. . . . There is another factor too. The competitive system absorbs the full energies of most of the people at all economic levels. Constant application, attention, and concentration of energy are the conditions of survival within it, primarily in the specifically economic professions, but also in other activities organized on their model. There is much less excess energy to be vented in war and conquest than in any precapitalist society. What excess energy there is flows largely into industry itself, accounts for its shining figures—the type of the captain of industry—and for the rest is applied to art, science, and the social struggle. In a purely capitalist world, what was once energy for war becomes simply energy for labor of every kind. Wars of conquest and adventurism in foreign policy in general are bound to be regarded as troublesome distractions, destructive of life's meaning, a diversion from the accustomed and therefore "true" task.

A purely capitalist world therefore can offer no fertile soil to imperialist impulses. That does not mean that it cannot still maintain an interest in imperialist expansion. . . . The point is that its people are likely to be essentially of an unwarlike disposition. Hence we must expect that anti-imperialist tendencies will show themselves wherever capitalism penetrates the economy and, through the economy, the mind of modern nations—most strongly, of course, where capitalism itself is strongest, where it has advanced furthest, encountered the least resistance, and preeminently where its types and hence democracy—in the "bourgeois" sense—come closest to political dominion. We must further expect that the types formed by capitalism will actually be the carriers of these tendencies. Is such the case? The facts that follow are cited to show that this expectation, which flows from our theory, is in fact justified.

1. Throughout the world of capitalism, and specifically among the elements formed by capitalism in modern social life, there has arisen a fundamental opposition to war, expansion, cabinet diplomacy, armaments, and socially entrenched professional armies. This opposition had its origin in the country that first turned capitalist—England— and arose coincidentally with that country's capitalist development. "Philosophical radicalism" was the first politically influential intel-

lectual movement to represent this trend successfully, linking it up, as was to be expected, with economic freedom in general and free trade in particular. . . .

2. Wherever capitalism penetrated, peace parties of such strength arose that virtually every war meant a political struggle on the domestic scene. The exceptions are rare—Germany in the Franco-Prussion war of 1870–1871, both belligerents in the Russo-Turkish war of 1877–1878. That is why every war is carefully justified as a defensive war by the governments involved, and by all the political parties, in their official utterances—indicating a realization that a war of a different nature would scarcely be tenable in a political sense. . . . In former times this would not have been necessary. Reference to an interest or pretense at moral justification was customary as early as the eighteenth century, but only in the nineteenth century did the assertion of attack, or the threat of attack, become the only avowed occasion for war. In the distant past, imperialism had needed no disguise whatever, and in the absolute autocracies only a very transparent one; but today imperialism is carefully hidden from public view—even though there may still be an unofficial appeal to warlike instincts. No people and no ruling class today can openly afford to regard war as a normal state of affairs or a normal element in the life of nations. No one doubts that today it must be characterized as an abnormality and a disaster. . . .

3. The type of industrial worker created by capitalism is always vigorously anti-imperialist. In the individual case, skillful agitation may persuade the working masses to approve or remain neutral—a concrete goal or interest in self-defense always playing the main part—but no initiative for a forcible policy of expansion ever emanates from this quarter. On this point official socialism unquestionably formulates not merely the interests but also the conscious will of the workers. Even less than peasant imperialism is there any such thing as socialist or other working-class imperialism.

4. Despite manifest resistance on the part of powerful elements, the capitalist age has seen the development of methods for preventing war, for the peaceful settlement of disputes among states. . . .

5. Among all capitalist economies, that of the United States is least burdened with precapitalist elements, survivals, reminiscences, and power factors. Certainly we cannot expect to find imperialist tendencies altogether lacking even in the United States, for the immigrants came from Europe with their convictions fully formed, and the environment certainly favored the revival of instincts of pugnacity. But we can conjecture that among all countries the United States is likely to exhibit the weakest imperialist trend. This turns out to be the truth. . . . In the course of the nineteenth century, the United States had numerous occasions for war, including instances that were well

calculated to test its patience. It made almost no use of such occasions. Leading industrial and financial circles in the United States had and still have an evident interest in incorporating Mexico into the Union. There was more than enough opportunity for such annexation—but Mexico remained unconquered. Racial catch phrases and working-class interests pointed to Japan as a possible danger. Hence possession of the Philippines was not a matter of indifference—yet surrender of this possession is being discussed. Canada was an almost defenseless prize—but Canada remained independent. . . .

These facts are scarcely in dispute. And since they fit into the picture of the mode of life which we have recognized to be the necessary product of capitalism, since we can grasp them adequately from the necessities of that mode of life and industry, it follows that capitalism is by nature anti-imperialist. Hence we cannot readily derive from it such imperialist tendencies as actually exist, but must evidently see them only as alien elements, carried into the world of capitalism from the outside, supported by non-capitalist factors in modern life. . . . The economic interest in the forcible conquest of India had to await free-booter personalities, in order to be followed up. In ancient Rome the domestic class interest in an expansive policy had to be seized upon by a vigorous, idle aristocracy, otherwise it would have been ruled out on internal political grounds. . . .

It may be stated as being beyond controversy that where free trade prevails *no* class has an interest in forcible expansion as such.[1] For in such a case the citizens and goods of every nation can move in foreign countries as freely as though those countries were politically their own—free trade implying far more than mere freedom from tariffs. In a genuine state of free trade, foreign raw materials and foodstuffs are as accessible to each nation as though they were within its own territory. Where the cultural backwardness of a region makes normal economic intercourse dependent on colonization, it does not matter, assuming free trade, which of the "civilized" nations undertakes the task of colonization. Dominion of the seas, in such a case, means little more than a maritime traffic police. Similarly, it is a matter of indifference to a nation whether a railway concession in a foreign country is acquired by one of its own citizens or not—just so long as the railway *is* built and put into efficient operation. For citizens of any country may use the railway, just like the fellow countrymen of its builder—while in the event of war it will serve whoever controls it in the military sense, regardless of who built it. It is true, of course, that profits and wages flowing from its construction

---

[1] [See John Gallagher and Ronald Robinson, "The Imperialism of Free Trade," in *The Economic History Review*, 2nd series, VI (Aug., 1953), 1–15, and Oliver MacDonagh, "The Anti-Imperialism of Free Trade," *ibid.*, XIV (April, 1962), 489–501.]

and operation will accrue, for the greater part, to the nation that built it. But capital and labor that go into the railway have to be taken from somewhere, and normally the other nations fill the gap. It is a fact that in a regime of free trade the essential advantages of international intercourse are clearly evident. The gain lies in the enlargement of the commodity supply by means of the division of labor among nations, rather than in the profits and wages of the export industry and the carrying trade. For these profits and wages would be reaped even if there were no export, in which case import, the necessary complement, would also vanish. Not even monopoly interests—if they existed—would be disposed toward imperialism in such a case. For under free trade only *international* cartels would be possible. . . .

*   *   *

This diagnosis also bears the prognosis of imperialism. The pre-capitalist elements in our social life may still have great vitality; special circumstances in national life may revive them from time to time; but in the end the climate of the modern world must destroy them. . . . And with them, imperialisms will wither and die.

It is not within the scope of this study to offer an ethical, esthetic, cultural, or political evaluation of this process. Whether it heals sores or extinguishes suns is a matter of utter indifference from the view-point of this study. It is not the concern of science to judge that. The only point at issue here was to demonstrate, by means of an important example, the ancient truth that the dead always rule the living.

Racism

After 1859, as Charles Darwin's *Origin of Species*, published in that year, was increasingly vulgarized, western Europeans began to speak of "lesser breeds" of men, of "survival of the fittest," and of the "law of tooth and claw." A nation, many argued, was like an organism that must grow or die. A race must retain its purity. An empire must bring the powerful and the pure to the weak and impure, so that the one might benefit the other. The sense of racial and cultural superiority thus generated often was made explicit, while even more often it was implicit, hidden under the rhetoric of the imperial administrators, who commented cruelly at times on the "natives."

Three short selections follow that illustrate this point. The first is from Sir Harry Johnston's *The Backward Peoples and Our Relations with Them*, published in 1920. Sir Harry was a British explorer who had been an important, and able, administrator in both Central and East Africa. The second, shorter, statement is by Sir James Brooke, the first White Rajah of Borneo—who had been the first European to settle successfully on that great island, and who was the first Civil Governor of Labuan—written to John C. Templer in 1841. The third selection is from the private journal of the *aide-de-camp* to Sir William Francis Drummond Jervois, who in 1875 was appointed British Governor of the Straits Settlements and charged with a number of complex negotiations with the sultans of the Malay peninsula.

From *The Backward Peoples and Our Relations with Them* by Sir Harry H. Johnston, The World of Today series (London: Oxford University Press, 1920), pp. 7–9. Reprinted by permission of the publisher.

Who Are the Backward Peoples?

. . . [L]et us proceed to define who and what these backward or unprogressive peoples are and to what extent they may be considered to be retrograde and ineffective as compared with the dominating white race. The chief and obvious distinction between the backward and the forward peoples is that the former, with the exception of about 20,000,000 in the Mediterranean basin and the Near East, are of coloured skin; while the latter are white-skinned or, as in the case of the Japanese and the inhabitants of Northern China, nearly white.

I think if we took all the factors into consideration—religion, education (especially knowledge concerning the relations between this planet and the universe of which it is a minute speck, the history and geography of the planet, the sciences that are a part of earth-study), standard of living, respect of sanitation, infant death rate, bodily strength, manner of government, regard for law and order, position in agriculture and manufactures,—we might appraise mathematically, according to the following ratio, the principal nations and peoples into which humanity is divided:—

1. Great Britain and Ireland, Canada and Newfoundland, White Australia, New Zealand, White South Africa (south of the Zambezi), Malta and Mauritius, United States, France, Corsica, much of Algeria and Tunis, Belgium and Luxembourg, Holland, Germany, Austria, Chekho-Slovakia, Italy, Switzerland, Hungary, Norway, Sweden, Denmark and Iceland, Finland, Esthonia, Spain, Chile, Argentina, Japan—100 per cent.
2. Poland and Lithuania, Serbia and Croatia, Bulgaria, Rumania, Portugal, Greece, Cyprus, Brazil, Peru, Colombia, British Guiana, French and Dutch Guiana, British and French West Indies, Cuba and Porto Rico, Hawaii, Uruguay—98 per cent.
3. Russia, Russian Siberia, Russian Central Asia, the Caucasus, Egypt, British India, French Indo-China, Siam, British Malaysia, Mexico, Central America, Bolivia, Venezuela, Ecuador, Paraguay, Java, Siam, Armenia—97 per cent.
4. Albania, Asia Minor, Morocco, Southern Algeria, Tripoli, Palestine, Syria, Persia, China, Tibet, Afghanistan, Zanzibar—95 per cent.
5. Madagascar, Black South Africa, French West Africa, British West Africa, Uganda, British Central and East Africa, Sumatra, Borneo, the Philippines, the Anglo-Egyptian Sudan, Angōla, Santo Domingo —90 per cent.
6. Abyssinia, Arabia, Portuguese East Africa, the Belgian Congo, Portuguese Congo, Liberia, Haiti, Celebes, Timor, New Caledonia, British Papua—80 per cent.
7. Dutch New Guinea and New Hebrides, Portuguese Guinea, French Central Africa—75 per cent.

This rough estimate of civilization and culture does not imply that the nations or peoples which are classed together resemble one another in all their stages of culture. Some will excell in one direction, some in another. In certain directions a people may be very forward, coupled with retrograde features which reduce their average value.

Obviously, the foremost nations in the world at the present day are Britain and the regions of the British Empire in which the white race predominates; the United States; France; and Germany,—not only by the numbers of their peoples and the degree of their national wealth, but by their industry, commerce and the proportion of educated to uneducated people in their population. In all elements of greatness, but not in potency of numbers, Denmark, Sweden, Norway, Finland, Holland, Luxembourg and Belgium, are on an equal footing. From their magnificent parts in history, one would like to class Spain, Portugal and Italy with these powers of the first rank, and before many more years have passed Spain and Italy, at any rate, may have attained such a position, when the whole of their peoples are sufficiently educated and political troubles have ceased to hinder progress.

It is the peoples of 95 per cent. to 90 per cent. that may be put in the unprogressive or retrograde class, unable at present to govern themselves in a manner conducive to progress; while those that are graded 80 and 75 per cent. still contain in their midst elements of sheer savagery. Such regions, if left alone by the controlling white man, might easily relapse into the unprofitable barbarism out of which they have been lifted with the white man's efforts during the past fifty years. . . .

> From *The Private Letters of Sir James Brooke, K.C.B., Rajah of Sarawak, Narrating the Events of His Life, from 1838 to the Present Time*, 3 vols., ed. John C. Templer (London: Richard Bentley, 1853), I, 114–15.

. . . The present sultan is imbecile, and Muda Hassim, on the death of his elder brother, succeeded to all the powers of the Bandharra or prime minister, and long exercised them till the following circumstances plunged him into his present position. The sultan's grandfather had an illegitimate son, by name Usop, uncle, of course, to the present sultan. This Pangeran Usop is by all accounts a restless, active, and ambitious Malay, and certainly far superior in energy to Muda Hassim. He came some six years ago to Sarawak, and for a sum of money, to be paid on delivery, agreed to make this country over to a brother of the sultan of Sambas. Muda Hassim would not consent to this, and Usop, to gain his end, roused the inhabitants here into rebellion, promising to assist them, which roused Muda Hassim to come here in person. The task was difficult, and his character is wanting in energy and promptness, though not deficient in sense. Once out of Borneo, Usop gained the weak sultan's ear, and has shaken his (Muda Hassim's) influence in the capital, and without my assistance, he certainly would have died in Sarawak. Now I have a moral influence here, which is surprising even to myself, and I have, what Englishmen all have, courage and energy, and Muda Hassim knows, that without my support he cannot stand here, and perhaps might fail likewise in Borneo; but the hitch is the mode of government. . . . Muda Hassim assures me there is no difficulty, and would fain leave the matter unsettled, which I will not consent to, *imprimis*, because he promised the contrary, and because we are on the Dutch boundary, and they will be apt to enquire into title. So we rest, but I think he will give way, chiefly from necessity, but he likewise is partial (and always has been) to Europeans in general, and to myself in particular. To-morrow or next day must decide one of these three things: first, whether I have the absolute and uncontrolled power; second, whether he makes a fair arrangement to repay me all my money and expenses; and thirdly, whether I shall attack him and take all and everything he has, and be off. The "lex talionis" is an alternative only in case of extreme necessity, and when it becomes apparent that he has been, and is, cheating and deceiving me. I give you leave, dear Jack, to ask what are the capabilities of this country, and how I am to support the expences till the capabilities are developed. I think I have before told you, that antimony ore is the staple commodity of this river. The antimony ore I shall retain in my own hands, and by holding a monopoly of it in the European markets, the price will never sink below 10*s*. a cwt., and will probably be higher. By this ore I shall derive a revenue of 1,800*l*. or 2,000*l*. a year, clear of expences of carriage, duty, commission, &c. There is besides a considerable quantity of gold. . . .

September 9th—[1875] Thursday. . . . At 12. An interview, the first of the series took place at which [were present] the Bandahara, the Mentri, the Sri Maharaja Lela, and the Laxamana.[1] The Bandahara is one of the poorest, feeblest specimens of humanity that can be imagined. There is a scared look about him and a wildness in his large eyes that confirms the assertions that have been made that he is a perfect maniac and that on occasion, retires to a corner of the room where he mews, shrieks & springs upon anybody passing. The Sri Maharajah Lela is a specimen of a thin half-starved bat. Very thin, very large prominent ears and a wizen face, his appearance was not calculated to show off the very shabby baju [shirt] and sarong which he was wearing. The Governor supported by his suite and with a guard of honour of service drawn up outside commenced the conversation, Mr. [Frank] Swettenham interpreting. . . .

[1] [This manuscript has not been published previously; it is in the editor's hands. In Perak the *Bandahara* was, in effect, the chief minister of state, the *Mentri* was a secretary of state, and the *Laxamana* the royal admiral. The office of *Maharaja Lela* was one of the eight chiefly offices, a group secondary to the four most important officials, and in 1874 it was held by the district chief of Pasir Salak. The *Temenggong* was the commander of the royal troops. It was at Pasir Salak that J. W. W. Birch, who was the first British Resident (an official advisory post), was killed, giving rise to the punitive expedition known as the Perak War. The *Mentri* and *Laxamana* were found to be implicated in Birch's death. Frank Swettenham escaped with his life during the uprising and eventually became Governor himself, in 1901. Jervois was transferred to South Australia in 1877.]

Coffee and syrup were then handed round and the meeting dissolved. [J.W.W.] Birch went across to the Bandahara's to see about the boats for the next-day and made every arrangement accordingly, a supply of food and money being given in addition. It had been stated that the Kota Lama men would not allow any white man to come to their village and they had threatened to fire upon Birch when he went up there some little time back. This village wh is some 2 miles above Qualla Kangsa [Kuala Kangsar] is the headquarters of the Temonggong and here live the Temonggong's two brothers who bear very indifferent characters. Birch landed there afterwards and burnt a house. Swettenham went there yesterday and found everything quiet and the people very civil. . . .

[November 5]. A sad trip this—leaving Singapore with the intention of proceeding to the Perak River to learn the circumstances of poor Birch's murder and the manner in which such murder should be revenged, whether the murder be connected with a general movement throughout the Peninsula to resist our control & active interference, an interference which the natives are now beginning to know what it means. . . .

Duty

Duty was seen in many guises. Was one's duty primarily to empire, to nation, to church, to the local inhabitants, or to oneself? However one viewed a sense of duty, during the height of the Victorian empire it generally meant speaking for those virtues which were taken to be uniquely British. These virtues were ably summed up as the "Little Things" that made for success, order, and progress, in Samuel Smiles's immensely influential books of self-help advice. Much impressed by Thomas Carlyle, the author of "The Nigger Question," Smiles was the British Horatio Alger, turning to thrift and self-help after exploring and finding a variety of collectivist theories and their applications inadequate. In 1859, the same year that *Origin of Species* was published, his famous *Self-Help* became available to the public; in 1871 *Character,* in 1875 *Thrift,* and in 1880 *Duty* followed. The third of these volumes, sub-titled *A Book of Domestic Counsel,* summarized the Victorian standards which helped gain, shape, and control the Empire. Smiles won great popularity abroad, especially in India, and into the 1950s *Thrift* in particular, from which the following material is drawn, continued to be a best-seller there. The attitudes expressed by Smiles may be compared to those of Hugh Clifford in his memorandum of 1922 for Nigeria (see pp. 128–133 below).

From *Thrift* by Samuel Smiles (London: [John Murray], 1875), pp. 136–39.

Neglect of small things is the rock on which the great majority of the human race have split. Human life consists of a succession of small events, each of which is comparatively unimportant, and yet the happiness and success of every man depends upon the manner in which these small events are dealt with. Character is built up on little things—little things well and honorably transacted. The success of a man in business depends upon his attention to little things. The comfort of a household is the result of small things well arranged and duly provided for. Good government can only be accomplished in the same way—by well-regulated provisions for the doing of little things.

Accumulations of knowledge and experience of the most valuable kind are the result of little bits of knowledge and experience carefully treasured up. Those who learn nothing or accumulate nothing in life, are set down as failures—because they have neglected little things. They may themselves consider that the world has gone against them; but in fact they have been their own enemies. There has long been a popular belief in "good luck"; but, like many other popular notions, it is gradually giving way. The conviction is extending that diligence is the mother of good luck; in other words, that a man's success in life will be proportionate to his efforts, to his industry, to his attention to small things. Your negligent, shiftless, loose fellows never meet with luck; because the results of industry are denied to those who will not use the proper efforts to secure them.

It is not luck, but labour, that makes men. Luck, says an American writer, is ever waiting for something to turn up; Labour, with keen eye and strong will, always turns up something. Luck lies in bed and wishes the postman would bring him news of a legacy; Labour turns out at six, and with busy pen or ringing hammer lays the foundation of a competence. Luck whines; Labour whistles. Luck relies on chance; Labour on character. Luck slips downwards to self-indulgence; Labour strides upward, and aspires to independence.

There are many little things in the household, attention to which is indispensable to health and happiness. Cleanliness consists in attention to a number of apparent trifles—the scrubbing of a floor, the dusting of a chair, the cleansing of a teacup—but the general result of the whole is an atmosphere of moral and physical well-being —a condition favourable to the highest growth of human character. The kind of air which circulates in a house may seem a small matter —for we cannot see the air, and few people know anything about it. Yet if we do not provide a regular supply of pure air within our houses, we shall inevitably suffer for our neglect. A few specks of dirt may seem neither here nor there, and a closed door or window would appear to make little difference; but it may make the difference of a life destroyed by fever; and therefore the little dirt and the little bad air are really very serious matters. The whole of the household regulations are, taken by themselves, trifles—but trifles tending to an important result.

A pin is a very little thing in an article of dress, but the way in which it is put into the dress often reveals to you the character of the wearer. A shrewd fellow was once looking out for a wife, and was on a visit to a family of daughters with this object. The fair one, of whom he was partially enamoured, one day entered the room in which he was seated with her dress partially unpinned, and her hair untidy: he never went back. You may say, such a fellow was "not worth a pin"; but he was really a shrewd fellow, and afterwards made a good husband. He judged of women as of men—by little things; and he was right.

A druggist advertised for an assistant, and he had applications from a score of young men. He invited them all to come to his shop at the same time, and set them each to make up a pennyworth of salts into a packet. He selected the one that did this little thing in the neatest and most expert manner. He inferred their general practical ability from their performance of this smallest bit of business.

Neglect of little things has ruined many fortunes and marred the best of enterprises. The ship which bore home the merchants' treasure was lost because it was allowed to leave the port from which it sailed with a very little hole in the bottom. For want of a nail the shoe of the aide-de-camp's horse was lost; for want of the shoe, the horse was lost; for want of the horse, the aide-de-camp himself was lost, for the enemy took him and killed him; and for want of the aide-de-camp's intelligence, the army of his general was lost: and all because a little nail had not been properly fixed in a horse's shoe!

"It will do!" is the common phrase of those who neglect little things. "It will do!" has blighted many a character, blasted many a fortune, sunk many a ship, burnt down many a house, and irretrievably ruined thousands of hopeful projects of human good. It always means stopping short of the right thing. It is a makeshift. It is a failure and defeat. Not what "will do," but what is the best possible thing to do, is the point to be aimed at! Let a man once adopt the maxim of "It will do," and he is given over to the enemy—he is on the side of incompetency and defeat—and we give him up as a hopeless subject! . . .

. . . When small things are habitually neglected, ruin is not far off. It is the hand of the diligent that maketh rich; and the diligent man or woman is attentive to small things as well as great. The things may appear very little and insignificant, yet attention to them is necessary as to matters of greater moment.

Take, for instance, the humblest of coins—a penny. What is the use of that little piece of copper—a solitary penny? What can it buy? Of what use is it? It is the price of a box of matches. It is only fit for giving to a beggar. And yet how much of human happiness depends upon the spending of the penny well.

A man may work hard, and earn high wages; but if he allows the pennies, which are the result of hard work, to slip out of his fingers —some going to the beer-shop, some this way, and some that—he will find that his life of hard work is little raised above that of animal drudgery. On the other hand, if he takes care of the pennies—putting some weekly into a benefit society or an insurance fund, others into a savings bank, and confides the rest to his wife to be carefully laid out, with a view to the comfortable maintenance and culture of his family—he will soon find that his attention to small matters will abundantly repay him, in increasing means, in comfort at home, and in a mind comparatively free from fears as to the future.

All savings are made up of little things. "Many a little makes a mickle." Many a penny makes a pound. A penny saved is the seed of pounds saved. And pounds saved mean comfort, plenty, wealth, and independence. But the penny must be earned honestly. It is said that a penny earned honestly is better than a shilling given. A Scotch proverb says, "The gear that is gifted is never sae sweet as the gear that is won." What though the penny be black? "The smith and his penny are both black." But the penny earned by the smith is an honest one. . . .

God

"Perhaps I shall die here," wrote a British traveling commissioner in The Gambia, "but I shall die a better man for having been here." "Fear nothing for me," said James Brooke in 1841, "the decision is in higher hands, and I am as willing to die, as live, in the present undertaking, if my death can benefit the poor people," the Dyaks of Borneo. Yet these same Dyaks were, according to Charles Kingsley, author of *Water Babies*—and no less Christian in his rhetoric than Brooke, with his desire to be a "guardian angel" in Sarawak—"the image of the beast . . . the enemies of Christ, the Prince of Peace. . . ."

The missionary often was a forerunner of more secular influences. Few could forget that while they spoke for God, their conception of Him assumed a nationality for His emissaries. Nor could the confusing variety of Christian groups agree upon how best to approach the savage. Provide him with the teaching of Christ, yes, but which teachings as interpreted by what groups? In many cases Protestant sects cooperated in order to extend Christianity, and Western ways, into the bush, but more often they found they could not agree upon the relative priorities of Western civilization, modern commerce, and Christian education. Their influence was great, for in many colonies they provided the only formal education available. Where Roman Catholic and Protestant met, or when a French missionary found himself among the same pagan men with a German or American mission group, native tribes often were taught something about the competitive ways of the West. Yet the Christian missions also brought much that was good, eliminating practices that only the most relativistic would not condemn, defending native interests (as in southern Africa) against the demands of the local white settlers, and bringing modern medicine with their prayer books. Puritanism, Old Testament theology, Darwinism, and a certain messianism that had its origin in national and racial pride, while promoting spiritual arrogance, also promoted good works. In 1857, the year of the Indian mutiny, a British missionary, Alexander Duff, attempted to explain the Indian hatred for the British and their rule. The first extract is from his book of letters and speeches published that year. The second selection, relating to Africa, is from the work of Captain Frederick Dealtry Lugard, who had been administrator of the East African Company from 1890 to 1892, and who in 1893 published *The Rise of Our East African Empire*.

From *The Indian Rebellion: Its Causes and Results, In a Series of Letters* by Alexander Duff (London: n.p., 1858), pp. 14–15.

. . . As regards the feelings of the great masses of the people towards the British Government, the most contradictory statements have been put forth. Here, as elsewhere, extremes will be found

wrong. That there ever was *anything like affection* or *loyal attachment*, in any true sense of these terms, on the part of any considerable portion of the native population towards the British power, is
what no one who really knows them could honestly aver. Individual
natives have become attached to individual Britons. Of the truth of
this statement even the recent sanguinary mutinies have furnished
some conspicuous examples. But such isolated facts can prove nothing as to the feelings generally prevalent with respect to the British
and their power. On the first subjugation or annexation of a province, the labouring classes, under a fresh sense of the manifold
tyrannies, exactions, and disorders from which they are delivered,
usually express satisfaction and delight. But as the first generation
dies out, and another rises up, knowing nothing but the even, steady,
continuous demands of the British authorities—demands which they
cannot evade, as they often might amid the weakness and turbulence
of native rule—they are apt to settle down into a state of necessitated
acquiescence, or sullen indifference, or latent disaffection and discontent—often secretly sighing for a change of rulers, that might give
them some chance of helping or bettering themselves. Such I believe
to be the general condition of the people of India, as regards their
feelings towards the British and their Government. And such being
their condition, any one might anticipate the evolution of conduct
which they might be expected to exhibit in the midst of a rebellion,
with what must appear to their minds its *doubtful issues*. The quieter
and more thoughtful spirits, under dread of ultimate retribution,
would hold back, or perhaps show favour or kindness to such Britons
as came in their way. The bolder, more resolute, and more impetuous
spirits, on the other hand, would at once be ready to sound a jubilee
of triumph over the downfall of the British power, and equally ready
to display the insolence of triumph over helpless and fugitive Britons.
And this I believe to be a tolerably exact picture of the state of feeling and conduct among the native population in the North-West
and Central Indian territories towards the British and their rule.

After escaping from the murderous hands of mutineers, British
gentlemen and ladies have, in particular instances, experienced kindness at the hands of the common villagers; but in far the greater
number of instances they have experienced *quite the reverse*. On this
account they have been constantly compelled to shun the villages
altogether, and betake themselves to jungles and pathless forests,
exposed to the attacks of beasts of prey, and to manifold privations,
the narration of which makes one almost shudder. And among the
murders ever and anon reported in our public journals, how often
do we find this entry opposite a name, *"Killed by the villagers!"*
. . . This very day, in one of our public journals, a gentleman, long
resident in the interior, thus writes: "I have lost all my property;

but my principal object is, to impress upon my countrymen (to convince the Government of this truth seems hopeless) the utter and most virulent hatred the natives have evinced throughout this outbreak, both to our Government and Europeans generally. In every instance where troops have mutinied, they have been joined by the inhabitants, not only of the bazaars, but of the towns and villages adjacent, who not only assisted the sepoys in burning, looting (plundering), and destroying Government property, and that of the European settlers, and all Christians, and in killing any of them they could. . . ."

Now, in the face of these, and scores of other substantially similar statements from all parts of the North-West and Central India, what becomes of the lullaby declarations of those who would fain persuade the British public that nowhere among the general civic or rural population of India does there exist any feeling of ill-will, or discontent, or disaffection, towards the British or their Government? All such unqualified declarations I do most solemnly regard as a gigantic (I do not say wilful) imposition on the British people. . . .

. . . It is but right that the British people, to whom the God of Providence has so mysteriously entrusted the sovereignty of this vast Indian empire, should know the real state of native feeling towards us and our power, that they may insist on a searching scrutiny into the causes which may have superinduced it, and, detecting the causes, may demand, as with a voice of thunder, some commensurate remedy. . . . Railways, and telegraphs, and irrigating canals, and other material improvements, *alone* will not do. Mere secular education, sharpening the intellect, and leaving the heart a prey to all the foulest passions and most wayward impulses, will not do. Mere legislation, which, in humanely prohibiting cruel rites and barbarous usages, goes greatly a-head of the darkened intelligence of the people, will not do. New settlements of the revenue, and landed tenures, however equitable in themselves, alone will not do. Ameliorations in the present monstrous system of police and corrupting machinery of law courts, however advantageous, alone will not suffice. A radical organic change in the structure of Government, such as would transfer it exclusively to the Crown, would not, could not, of itself furnish an adequate cure for our deep-seated maladies.

No, no! Perhaps the present earthquake shock which has passed over Indian society, upheaving and tearing to shreds some of the noblest monuments of material civilisation, as well as the most improved expedients of legislative and administrative wisdom, has been permitted, to prove that all merely human plans and systems whatsoever, that exclude the life-awakening, elevating, purifying doctrines of gospel grace and salvation, have impotence and failure stamped on their wrinkled brows. Let, then, the Christian people of the highly-favoured British isles, . . . rise up, . . . let them decree . . .

that henceforward those commissioned by them to rule over and administer justice to the millions of this land shall not dare, in their public acts and proclamations, practically to ignore or scornfully repudiate the very name and faith of Jesus. . . .

From *The Rise of Our East African Empire* . . . by Frederick Dealtry (later Lord) Lugard (Edinburgh: William Blackwood & Sons Ltd., 1893), pp. 73–75.

One word as regards missionaries themselves. The essential point in dealing with Africans is to establish a respect for the European. Upon this—the prestige of the white man—depends his influence, often his very existence, in Africa. If he shows by his surroundings, by his assumption of superiority, that he is far above the native, he will be respected, and his influence will be proportionate to the superiority he assumes and bears out by his higher accomplishments and mode of life. In my opinion—at any rate with reference to Africa—it is the greatest possible mistake to suppose that a European can acquire a greater influence by adopting the mode of life of the natives. In effect, it is to lower himself to their plane, instead of elevating them to his. The sacrifice involved is wholly unappreciated, and the motive would be held by the savage to be poverty and lack of social status in his own country. The whole influence of the European in Africa is gained by this assertion of a superiority which commands the respect and excites the emulation of the savage. To forego this vantage-ground is to lose influence for good. I may add, that the loss of prestige consequent on what I should term the humiliation of the European affects not merely the missionary himself, but is subversive of all efforts for secular administration, and may even invite insult, which may lead to disaster and bloodshed. To maintain it a missionary must, above all things, be a gentleman; for no one is more quick to recognize a real gentleman than the African savage. He must at all times assert himself, and repel an insolent familiarity, which is a thing entirely apart from friendship born of respect and affection. His dwelling house should be as superior to those of the native as he is himself superior to them. And this, while adding to his prestige and influence, will simultaneously promote his own health and energy, and so save money spent on invalidings to England, and replacements due to sickness or death. . . .

I am convinced that the indiscriminate application of such precepts as those contained in the words to "turn the other cheek also to the smiter," and to be "the servant of all men," is to wholly misunderstand and misapply the teaching of Christ. The African holds

the position of a late-born child in the family of nations, and must
as yet be schooled in the discipline of the nursery. He is neither the
intelligent ideal crying out for instruction, and capable of appreciat-
ing the subtle beauties of Christian forbearance and self-sacrifice,
which some well-meaning missionary literature would lead us to
suppose; nor yet, on the other hand, is he universally a rampant can-
nibal, predestined by Providence to the yoke of the slave, and fitted
for nothing better, as I have elsewhere seen him depicted. . . .
That is to say, that there is in him, like the rest of us, both good and
bad, and that the innate good is capable of being developed by
culture. . . .

Science

The new science taught that man could and must be classified, that social evolution would determine the course of the future, and that genetics could be controlled to a considerable degree. Men calling themselves scientists measured cranial capacity, genital size, the length of arms and legs, the amount of uric acid in human waste, and found one people "higher" or "lower" on some "scientific" scale. During World War I a body of French scientists seriously argued that German spies could be detected through urinanalysis, and as late as the 1950s a famed historian suggested that certain peoples—the Polynesians and the Jews, for example—were suspended on a plateau, their progress being less vigorous than that of other, more efficient groups. The notion that quantification would help provide bridges between people was less strong than the corresponding but opposing notion that quantification would show the great chasms between peoples. The following statements come, first, from Sir Thomas Munro, who was Governor of Madras from 1820 until 1827, and second, from Benjamin Kidd's famous and much-quoted work, *Social Evolution*, published in 1894. The third statement is from Herman Merivale, who was Drummond Professor of Political Economy in Oxford University between 1837 and 1842 (and later a Permanent Under-Secretary in the Colonial Office and head of the India Office) and who—in the university lecture upon which the selection draws—used the biological metaphors common to all nineteenth-century theorists of Empire. The last is from one of the most influential books of the midcentury, Sir Charles Wentworth Dilke's *Greater Britain*, first published in London in 1868.

From *Major General Sir Thomas Munro, Selections from His Minutes and Other Official Writings*, 2 vols., ed. Sir Alexander J. Arbuthnot (London: Routledge & Kegan Paul, Ltd., 1881), II, 70.

. . . When we compare other countries with England, we usually speak of England as she is now—we scarcely ever think of going back beyond the Reformation; and we are apt to regard every foreign country as ignorant and uncivilized, whose state of government does not in some degree approximate to our own, even though it should be higher than our own was at no very distant period.

We should look upon India, not as a temporary possession, but as one which is to be maintained permanently, until the natives shall in some future age have abandoned most of their superstitions and prejudices, and become sufficiently enlightened to frame a regular government for themselves, and to conduct and preserve it. Whenever such a time shall arrive, it will probably be best for both countries that the British control over India should be gradually with-drawn. That the desirable change here contemplated may in some after age be effected in India, there is no cause to despair. Such a change was at one time in Britain itself at least as hopeless as it is here. When we reflect how much the character of nations has always been influenced by that of governments, and that some, once the most cultivated, have sunk into barbarism, while others, formerly the rudest, have attained the highest point of civilization, we shall see no reason to doubt that if we pursue steadily the proper meas-ures, we shall in time so far improve the character of our Indian subjects as to enable them to govern and protect themselves.

From *Social Evolution* by Benjamin Kidd (London: Methuen & Company, Ltd., 1894), pp. 318–21. Reprinted by permission of the publisher.

. . . Exceptionally influenced as the British nation has been by the altruistic spirit underlying our civilisation, its administration of the Indian peninsula has never been marked by those features which distinguished Spanish rule in the American continent. English rule has tended more and more to involve the conscientious discharge of the duties of our position towards the native races. We have respected their rights, their ideas, their religions, and even their independence to the utmost extent compatible with the efficient administration of the government of the country.

The result has been remarkable. There has been for long in prog-ress in India a steady development of the resources of the country which cannot be paralleled in any other tropical region of the world. Public works on the most extensive scale and of the most per-manent character have been undertaken and completed; roads and bridges have been built; mining and agriculture have been developed; irrigation works, which have added considerably to the fertility and resources of large tracts of country, have been constructed; even san-itary reform is beginning to make considerable progress. European enterprise too, attracted by security and integrity in the government, has been active. Railways have been gradually extended over the Peninsula. Indian tea, almost unknown a short time ago has, through the planting and cultivation of suitable districts under European supervision, already come into serious competition with the Chinese article in the markets of the world. The cotton industry of India has already entered on friendly rivalry with that of Lancashire. Other industries, suited to the conditions of the country, are in like manner rising into prominence, without any kind of artificial protection or encouragement; the only contribution of the ruling powers to their welfare being the guarantee of social order and the maintenance of the conditions of efficiency and integrity in the administration of the departments of government.

The commerce of the country has expanded in a still more striking manner. In the largest open market in the world, that which Great Britain provides, India now stands third on the list as contributor of produce, ranking only below the United States and France, and above Germany and all our Australian colonies together. She takes, too, as much as she gives, for her exports to and imports from the United Kingdom nearly balance each other. In the character of importer she is, indeed, the largest of all the customers of Great Britain, our Australasian colonies and the United States coming after her on the list. . . .

Very different . . . is the spirit animating both sides in [the] development of the resources of India as compared with that which prevailed in past times. There is no question now of the ruling race merely exploiting India to their own selfish advantage. Great Britain desires to share in the prosperity she has assisted in creating, it is true; but, for the most part, she shares indirectly and in participation with the rest of the world. India sends her products to British markets, but she is equally free to send them elsewhere. As her development proceeds she offers a larger market for the products of our industries; but England has reserved to herself no exclusive advantages in Indian markets. Under the principle of free trade all the rest of the world may compete with her on equal terms in those markets. Our gain tends to be a gain, not only to India, but to civilisation in general.

The object-lesson that all this has afforded has not been without its effect on English public opinion—an effect which deepens as the true nature of the relationship existing between the two countries is more generally understood. Nor is there lack of similar experiences elsewhere. The work undertaken by France in Algeria and Tunis, although it has differed in many important respects from that performed by Great Britain in India, and although it has been undoubtedly more directly inspired by the thought of immediate benefit to French interests, has been on the whole, it must be frankly confessed, work done in the cause of civilisation in general. Within the past decade we have had a more striking lesson still in the case of Egypt. Some seventeen years ago that country, although within sight of, and in actual contact with, European civilisation, had reached a condition of disaster through misgovernment, extravagance, and oppression without example, as a recent writer, who speaks with authority, has insisted, "in the financial history of any country from the remotest ages to the present time." Within thirteen years the public debt of a country of only 6 millions of inhabitants had been increased from 3 millions to 89 millions, or nearly thirty-fold. With a submissive population, a corrupt bureaucracy, and a reckless, ambitious, and voluptuous ruler, surrounded by adventurers of every kind, we had all the elements of national bankruptcy and ruin. Things drifted from bad to worse, but it was felt that nothing could be more at variance, theoretically, with the principles of the Liberal party then in power in England, than active interference by the English people in the affairs of that country. Yet within a few years circumstances had proved stronger than prevailing views, and England found herself most unwillingly compelled to interfere by force in the government of Egypt. . . .

From *Lectures on Colonization and Colonies* by Herman Merivale (London: Longmans, Green and Company, Ltd., 1861), pp. 204–6.

The mere effort of directing the mind to travel abroad to those new regions of romance and expectation, where all is life, and hope, and active energy, affords a relief to the spirits, which again feel wearied and fettered when it is called back to fix its attention at home. This yearning after the distant and the unseen is a common propensity of our nature; and how much is the force of that "secret impulse" cherished and strengthened, in the minds of us Englishmen, by all the associations in the midst of which we are educated! Masters of every sea, and colonists of every shore, there is scarcely a nook which our industry has not rendered accessible, scarcely a region to which the eye can wander in the map, in which we have not some object of national interest—some factory for our trade, some settlement of our citizens. It is a sort of instinctive feeling to us all, that the destiny of our name and nation is not here, in this narrow island which we occupy; that the spirit of England is volatile, not fixed; that it lives in our language, our commerce, our industry, all those channels of intercommunication by which we embrace and connect the vast multitude of states, both civilised and uncivilised, throughout the world. No circumstance, in my view, affords at once such a proof of our vocation to this great end, and such an augury of our success in the pursuit of it, as the peculiar and (in a certain sense of the word) unselfish interest with which schemes of colonization are regarded by almost all classes of society; the sanguine hopes we are apt to entertain of their success, the sacrifices we are willing to make for their promotion, even with little or no regard to the manner in which they may affect our economical prosperity at home.

Surely, few things are more important to the welfare of an infant nation than to be impressed with a sense of its own permanent existence—its own nationality, so to speak—by the evidence of institutions rooted as it were in the soil, and protected by the same safe-guard with which the constitution fences the property of individuals and the sovereignty of the monarch. The situation of a modern colonist is very different from that which imagination rather than history suggests, when we carry our minds back to the foundation of states and empires. He comes from an old country, his habits regulated by its usages, his mind full of its institutions. Perhaps he is strongly attached to those institutions: perhaps he is discontented with them. But, in either case, his strongest impressions, his most vehement emotions, are connected with them. He lives mentally in the past and future rather than the present, in the society which he has left, and that of which he dreams as a distant possibility, rather than that which he contributes to create. He regards the immediate social prospects of the new community, as such, at first with comparative indifference; it is the home of his industry, not of his thoughts: he cares little about its development from within; but all his old party feelings are excited in furthering or in opposing the transplantation of laws and establishments from the mother country. And these feelings are inherited by his descendants for many generations; their strength diminishes very gradually. . . .

The consequence of this is, a tendency in new colonial communities to allow those institutions which are of domestic origin to grow up carelessly and at random; to frame laws merely for actual emergencies; to fill up the foundations with rubbish, and let future generations care for the finished building. There are some who believe such improvised and practical institutions to be the best of all, or rather the only useful ones. But those who contemplate national establishments not merely with a view to their immediate adaptation for use, but as contributing most essentially, among other causes, to form the mind and temper of the people itself, cannot but think that it is well to commence the building with some reference to a preconceived idea, not inflexible indeed, but still independent, and to give pledges, as it were, to the future, binding the people to revere and guard the durable elements of moral greatness. Nothing could tend more decidedly towards imparting the requisite fixity and self-existence to colonial societies, than to place on a permanent footing endowments for education, both for popular schools and colleges. And, the same would be true in a still higher degree of a national church establishment, if that establishment could really comprehend the mass of the community.

May we not conceive England as retaining the seat of the chief executive authority, the prescriptive reverence of her station, the superiority belonging to her vast accumulated wealth, and as the commercial metropolis of the world; and united, by these ties only, with a hundred nations,—not unconnected, like those which yielded to the spear of the Roman, but her own children, owning one faith and one language? May we not figure to ourselves, scattered thick as stars over the surface of this earth, communities of citizens owning the name of Britons, bound by allegiance to a British sovereign, and uniting heart and hand in maintaining the supremacy of Britain on every shore which her unconquered flag can reach? . . .

> From *Greater Britain: A Decade of Travel in English-Speaking Countries during 1866–7* by Charles Wentworth Dilke (Philadelphia: Lippincott & Co., 1869), I, 329–30.

The case of the flies is plain enough. The Maori and the English fly live on the same food, and require about the same amount of warmth and moisture: the one which is best fitted to the common conditions will gain the day, and drive out the other. The English fly has had to contend not only against other English flies, but against every fly of temperate climates: we have traded with every land, and brought the flies of every clime to England. The English fly is the best possible fly of the whole world, and will naturally beat down and exterminate, or else starve out, the merely provincial Maori fly. . . .

Natural selection is being conducted by nature in New Zealand on a grander scale than any we have contemplated, for the object of it here is man. In America, in Australia, the white man shoots or poisons his red or black fellow, and exterminates him through the workings of superior knowledge; but in New Zealand it is peacefully, and without extraordinary advantages, that the Pakéha[1] beats his Maori brother.

---

[1] [White settler in New Zealand.]

Part Three

 METHODS

As we have seen, expansion was the product of a variety of motives, and control over virtually the whole of Africa and the Pacific, much of Asia, and, for a time, all of the New World was achieved in numerous ways. Many of the methods for acquiring territory, suzerainty, trade concessions, and alliances had to be given formal status by treaty, agreement, or international convention. One may best judge the legality of imperial expansion, its various methods, and the types of control exercised by the European powers through an examination of representative, and for the most part semi-public, statements such as those that follow. Spheres of influence, political control, economic privileges—all were imposed, or negotiated, with an assumption that the same interests were shared by both native people and imperial overlord, or by the foreign offices of two separate states.

Spheres of Influence

Early in 1819 Stamford Raffles arranged with the sultan and Temenggong of Johore, who had been installed by the British shortly before, to have exclusive access to the island of Singapore for British factories, and in return both men were to be paid annual allowances. All other nations—and most particularly the Dutch, who from Java had dominated trade in the area—were to be excluded. Raffles had acted without full authorization, however, and in London and The Hague the arrangement had to be given a more formal basis. The result was the Treaty of London, signed in 1824, by which the Dutch accepted British occupancy rights at Singapore and agreed to the Straits of Singapore as a general demarcation to the spheres of influence of the two nations in the spice islands. The chief articles of the treaty follow.

From *Malaysia: Selected Historical Readings,* compiled by John Bastin and Robin W. Winks (Kuala Lumpur: Oxford University Press, 1966), pp. 134–36. Copyright © 1966 by Oxford University Press.

Article II

The Subjects and Vessels of one Nation shall not pay, upon importation or exportation, at the Ports of the other in the Eastern Seas, any Duty at a rate beyond the double of that at which the Subjects and Vessels of the Nation to which the Port belongs are charged.

The Duties paid on exports or imports at a British Port on the Continent of India, or in Ceylon, on Dutch bottoms, shall be arranged so as, in no case, to be charged at more than double the amount of the Duties paid by British Subjects and on British bottoms.

In regard to any article upon which no Duty is imposed, when imported or exported by the Subjects, or on the Vessels, of the Nation to which the Port belongs, the Duty charged upon the Subjects or Vessels of the other shall in no case, exceed six per cent.

Article III

The High Contracting Parties engage, that no Treaty hereafter made by Either, with any Native Power in the Eastern Seas, shall

contain any Article tending, either expressly, or by the imposition
of unequal Duties to exclude the Trade of the other Party from the
Ports of such Native Power: and that if in any Treaty now existing
on either Part any Article to that effect has been admitted, such
Article shall be abrogated upon the conclusion of the present Treaty.

It is understood that, before the conclusion of the present Treaty,
communication has been made by each of the Contracting Parties to
the other, of all Treaties or Engagements subsisting between each
of Them, respectively, and any Native Power in the Eastern Seas;
and that the like communication shall be made of all such Treaties
concluded by Them, respectively, hereafter.

*   *   *

Article VI

It is agreed that Order shall be given by the Two Governments
to Their Officers and Agents in the East, not to form any new Settlement on any of the Islands in the Eastern Seas, without previous
Authority from their respective Governments in Europe.

Article VII

The Molucca Islands, and especially Amboyna, Banda, Ternate,
and their immediate Dependencies, are excepted from the operation
of the . . . II, III . . . Articles, until the Netherland Government
shall think fit to abandon the monopoly of Spices; but if the said
Government shall, at any time previous to such abandonment of the
monopoly, allow the Subjects of any Power, other than a Native
Asiatic Power, to carry on any Commercial Intercourse with the said
Islands, the Subjects of His Brittannick Majesty shall be admitted to
such Intercourse, upon a footing precisely similar.

Article VIII

His Netherland Majesty cedes to His Britannick Majesty all his
establishments on the Continent of India; and renounces all privileges
and exemptions enjoyed or claimed in virtue of those Establishments.

Article IX

The Factory of Fort Marlborough and all the English Possessions on the Island of Sumatra, are hereby ceded to His Netherland Majesty and His Britannick Majesty further engages that no British Settlement shall be formed on that Island, nor any Treaty concluded by British Authority, with any Native Prince, Chief, or State therein.

Article X

The Town and Fort of Malacca, and its Dependencies, are hereby ceded to His Britannick Majesty; and His Netherland Majesty engages, for Himself and his Subjects, never to form any Establishment on any part of the Peninsula of Malacca, or to conclude any Treaty with any Native Prince, Chief, or State therein.

Article XI

His Britannick Majesty withdraws the objections which have been made to the occupation of the Island of Billiton and its Dependencies, by the Agents of the Netherland Government.

Article XII

His Netherland Majesty withdraws the objections which have been made to the occupation of the Island of Singapore, by the Subjects of His Britannick Majesty.

His Britannick Majesty, however, engages, that no British Establishment shall be made on the Carimon Isles, or on the Islands of Battam, Bintang, Lingin, or on any of the other Islands South of the Straits of Singapore, nor any Treaty concluded by British authority with the Chiefs of those Islands.

*   *   *

Article XV

The High Contracting Parties agree that none of the Territories or Establishments mentioned in Articles VIII, IX, X, XI, and XII shall be, at any time, transferred to any other Power. In case of any of the said Possessions being abandoned by one of the present Contracting Parties, the right of occupation thereof shall immediately pass to the other.

Negotiations with Native Peoples

One difficulty confronting the European powers lay in the need to discover who spoke with authority for native groups. Tribes were organized socially, and even politically, in ways that often varied substantially from place to place. A treaty concluded with one native chief might not hold for the entire tribe for which it was assumed that he could speak; it almost certainly would not hold for other tribes. When possible, the Europeans preferred to treat directly with councils of chiefs who might speak for an entire people. Even when they did so, however, certain tribes were almost certain to be omitted, and misunderstandings arose. One such treaty was that negotiated on behalf of the Crown with the United Tribes of New Zealand, the Maori, at Waitangi, in 1840. This, the Treaty of Waitangi, would be the basis for European (or *pakeha*) settlement upon the land in New Zealand's North Island.

Her Majesty Queen Victoria, Queen of the United Kingdom of Great Britain and Ireland, regarding with Her Royal favour the Native Chiefs and Tribes of New Zealand, and anxious to protect their just Rights and Property, and to secure to them the enjoyment of Peace and Good Order, has deemed it necessary, in consequence of the great number of Her Majesty's Subjects who have already settled in New Zealand, and the rapid extension of Emigration both from Europe and Australia which is still in progress, to constitute and appoint a functionary properly authorized to treat with the Aborigines of New Zealand for the recognition of Her Majesty's Sovereign Authority over the whole or any part of those Islands. Her Majesty, therefore, being desirous to establish a settled form of Civil Government with a view to avert the evil consequences which must result from the absence of the necessary Laws, and Institutions alike to the Native population and to her Subjects, has been graciously pleased to empower and authorise me, William Hobson, a Captain in Her Majesty's Royal Navy, Consul, and Lieutenant-Governor of such parts of New Zealand as may be, or hereafter shall be, ceded to Her Majesty, to invite the confederated and independent Chiefs of New Zealand to concur in the following Articles and Conditions.

Article the First

The Chiefs of the Confederation of the United Tribes of New Zealand and the separate and independent Chiefs who have not become members of the Confederation, cede to Her Majesty the Queen of England, absolutely and without reservation, all the rights and powers of Sovereignty which the said Confederation or Individual Chiefs respectively exercise or possess, or may be supposed to exercise or to possess, over their respective Territories as the sole Sovereigns thereof.

Article the Second

Her Majesty the Queen of England confirms and guarantees to the Chiefs and Tribes of New Zealand, and to the respective families and individuals thereof, the full, exclusive, and undisturbed possession of their Lands and Estates, Forests, Fisheries and other properties which they may collectively or individually possess, so long as it is their wish and desire to retain the same in their possession; but the Chiefs of the United Tribes and the Individual Chiefs yield to Her Majesty the exclusive right of Pre-emption over such Lands as the proprietors thereof may be disposed to alienate, at such prices as may be agreed between the respective proprietors and persons appointed by Her Majesty to treat with them in that behalf.

Article the Third

In consideration thereof Her Majesty the Queen of England extends to the Natives of New Zealand Her Royal protection and imparts to them all the Rights and Privileges of British subjects.

W[illiam] Hobson
Lieutenant-Governor

Now therefore, we, the Chiefs of the Confederation of the United Tribes of New Zealand, being assembled in Congress, at Victoria, in Waitangi, and we, the Separate and Independent Chiefs of New

Zealand, claiming authority over the Tribes and Territories which are specified under our respective names, having been made fully to understand the provisions of the foregoing Treaty, accept and enter into the same in the full spirit and meaning thereof.

In Witness whereof, we have attached our signatures or marks at the places and dates respectively specified.

Done at Waitangi, this 6th day of February, in the year of our Lord 1810.

Tribal Treaties

One might not be successful in negotiating an agreement with an entire native people. Piecemeal, the imperial nation could nonetheless acquire substantial rights from specific tribes, the boundaries of which would be unclear. The Royal Niger Company, in its efforts to acquire rights in the valley of the Niger River, used blank treaties such as the following.

From *The Map of Africa by Treaty*, 2nd and revised edition, I, *Abysinnia to Great Britain (Colonies)* by Sir Edward Hertslet (London: Her Majesty's Stationery Office, 1896), 467–68.

We, the undersigned Chiefs of _____, with the view to the bettering of the condition of our country and people, do this day cede to the Royal Niger Company (Chartered and Limited), for ever, the whole of our territory extending from _____.

We also give to the said Royal Niger Company (Chartered and Limited) full power to settle all native disputes arising from any cause whatever, and we pledge ourselves not to enter into any war with other tribes without the sanction of the said Royal Niger Company (Chartered and Limited).

We understand that the said Royal Niger Company (Chartered and Limited) have full power to mine, farm, and build in any portion of our country.

We bind ourselves not to have any intercourse with any strangers or foreigners except through the said Royal Niger Company (Chartered and Limited).

In consideration of the foregoing, the said Royal Niger Company (Chartered and Limited) bind themselves not to interfere with any of the native laws or customs of the country, consistently with the maintenance of order and good government.

The said Royal Niger Company (Chartered and Limited) agree to pay native owners of land a reasonable amount for any portion they may require.

The said Royal Niger Company (Chartered and Limited) bind themselves to protect the said Chiefs from the attacks of any neighbouring aggressive tribes.

The said Royal Niger Company (Chartered and Limited) also agree to pay the said Chiefs _____ measures native value.

We, the undersigned witnesses, do hereby solemnly declare that the _____ Chiefs whose names are placed opposite their respective crosses have in our presence affixed their crosses of their own free will and consent, and that the said _____ has in our presence affixed his signature.

Done in triplicate at _____, this _____ day of _____, 188__.

✼   ✼   ✼

Declaration by Interpreter.

I, _____, of _____, do hereby solemnly declare that I am well acquainted with the language of the _____ country, and that on the _____ day of _____, 188__, I truly and faithfully explained the above Agreement to all the Chiefs present, and that they understood its meaning.

Displacing Troublesome Rulers

On occasion local rulers would prove uncooperative. They might then be deposed, as shown by the following document—by which Lord Dalhousie removed the Maharajah Dhulip Singh Bahadoor of the Punjab. In 1849 his lands were annexed to the East India Company, and Queen Victoria acquired a famous jewel.

From *The Life of the Marquis of Dalhousie* by Sir William Lee-Warner (London: Macmillan and Co., Ltd., 1904), I, 242–43.

Terms granted to the Maharajah Dulleep Sing Bahadoor, on the part of the Honorable East India Company, by Henry Meirs Elliot, Esq., Foreign Secretary to the Government of India, and Lieutenant-Colonel Sir Henry Montgomery Lawrence, K.C.B., Resident, in virtue of full powers vested in them by the Right Honorable James, Earl of Dalhousie, Knight of the Most Ancient and Most Noble Order of the Thistle, one of her Majesty's most Honorable Privy Council, Governor-General appointed by the Honorable East India Company to direct and control all their affairs in the East Indies, and accepted on the part of his Highness the Maharajah, by Rajah Tej Sing, Rajah Deena Nath, Bhaee Nidham Sing, Fukeer Noorooddeen, Gundur Sing, Agent of Sirdar Shere Sing Sindhanwalla, and Sirdar Lall Sing, Agent and son of Sirdhar Utter Sing Kaleanwalla, Members of the Council of Regency, invested with full power and authority on the part of His Highness.

1st.—His Highness the Mah[a]rajah Dulleep Sing shall resign for himself, his heirs, and his successors, all right, title, and claim to the sovereignty of the Punjab, or to any sovereign power whatever.

2nd.—All the property of the State, of whatever description and wheresoever found, shall be confiscated to the Honorable East India Company, in part payment of the debt due by the State of Lahore to the British Government, and of the expenses of the war.

3rd.—The gem called the Koh-i-noor, which was taken from Shah Shoojaool-Moolk by Maharajah Runjeet Sing, shall be surrendered by the Maharajah of Lahore to the Queen of England.

4th.—His Highness Dulleep Sing shall receive from the Honorable East India Company, for the support of himself, his relatives, and the servants of the State, a pension not less than four and not exceeding five lakhs[1] of Company's rupees per annum.

---

[1] [A *lakh* was, usually, one hundred thousand.]

5th.—His Highness shall be treated with respect and honour. He shall retain the title of Maharajah Dulleep Sing Bahadoor, and he shall continue to receive, during his life, such portion of the above-named pension as may be allotted to himself personally, provided he shall remain obedient to the British Government, and shall reside at such place as the Governor-General of India may select.

Granted and accepted at Lahore, on the 29th of March, 1849, and ratified by the Right Honorable and Governor-General on the 5th April, 1849.

Trading Privileges

The following instructions, prepared by Lord Palmerston, the British Colonial Secretary, for Her Majesty's Consul, John Beecroft, with respect to his mission to Abeokuta, in what is today Nigeria, illustrate the steps by which penetration took place.

From *Hansard's Parliamentary Papers*, 1852, LIV, no. 221, 346–48.

I now proceed to give you instructions for your mission to Abbeokuta. . . .

A short time since a deputation from the Church Missionary Society waited upon me, and represented among other things that the establishment of commercial relations with the interior of Africa through the Yoruba tribe, would materially contribute to the suppression of the Slave Trade, and that if free and secure navigation on the Ogu could be obtained, most of the advantages which were proposed by the expedition of the Niger in 1842 would be attained; that traders from the banks of the Niger visit the principal markets of Abbeokuta; and that there is little doubt that the road to Egba and Rabbah, the former of which was the highest point reached by the Niger expedition, might be opened for trade through the Ogu River.

Abbeokuta, as I am informed, is the chief town of the Egba province of the Yoruba Kingdom, and contains above 50,000 inhabitants. It is situated upon the east bank of the Ogu, and that river is navigable for canoes to within a mile of Abbeokuta, and discharges itself into the sea at the Island of Lagos. Lagos is therefore said to be the natural port of Abbeokuta; but the Slave Trade being carried on at Lagos with great activity, the Yoruba people have been obliged to use the port of Badagry, between which and Abbeokuta communications are carried on by a difficult road by land.

But besides the impediments which the slave-dealers at Lagos throw in the way of legitimate commerce, the Yoruba people experience another hindrance to their prosperity, and a constant cause of alarm from the hostility of the King of Dahomey, who harasses them by an annual slave-hunt, and who is said to have threatened the destruction of the town of Abbeokuta. His enmity is said to be especially excited by the fact that the Yorubas are becoming prosperous and are gaining wealth by their commerce with the English, and by refraining from Slave Trade.

The Yorubas are represented to be a commercial people in their habits, and much trade has been carried on between Abbeokuta and Sierra Leone, by way of Badagry. It is also believed that many of the liberated Africans[1] have emigrated from Sierra Leone to Abbeokuta, and many vessels owned entirely by liberated Africans are said to be employed in the Trade between Sierra Leone and Badagry. There is also a regular trade carried on between London and Badagry. English missionaries have been received both at Badagry and Abbeokuta with great kindness, and their valuable services in imparting religious instruction and in promoting social improvements appear to be duly appreciated by the natives. The people of Abbeokuta are said to feel a strong desire that the Slave Trade should be wholly abolished, and that legitimate traffic should be substituted for it; and the Egba chiefs manifest a favourable disposition towards the English nation.

Under these circumstances, Her Majesty's Government have deemed it advisable that you should at a suitable season visit Abbeokuta, in order to ascertain by inquiry on the spot, the actual wants, and wishes, and disposition of the Yoruba people.

I have accordingly to instruct you to proceed on this mission as soon as you conveniently can. Before you proceed, however, to Abbeokuta, it will be advisable that you should first visit the chiefs on the coast within your Consular jurisdiction, and that you should endeavour to ascertain the sentiments and intentions of such of them as have not already entered into amicable relations with Great Britain.

You will explain to those chiefs what is stated in my letters addressed to the chiefs themselves, that the principal object of your appointment is to encourage and promote legitimate and peaceful commerce, whereby those chiefs and their people may obtain in exchange for the products of their own country, those European commodities which they may want for their own use and enjoyment; so that the great natural resources of their country may be developed, their wealth and their comforts increased, and the practice of stealing, buying, and selling men, women, and children, may be put an end to; and you will impress upon their minds that it is the earnest desire of the Queen's Government to contribute in every possible way to their welfare and prosperity, if they will but listen favourably to your overtures, and will honestly follow the friendly counsel which is offered to them by the British Government.

When by personal communication with these chiefs, you shall have made yourself acquainted with their disposition, and shall have ascertained how far they may be inclined to break off their connexion with slave-dealers, and to apply themselves to legitimate trade, you will be the better prepared to undertake with advantage your mission to Abbeokuta.

[1] [Freed slaves taken to live in Sierra Leone.]

With respect to any aggressive intentions of the King of Dahomey towards the Yoruba people, you will have an opportunity, during your visit to Abomey, to bring that subject under the notice of the King; you will represent to him that the people who dwell in the Yoruba and Popo Countries are the friends of England, and that the British Government takes a great interest in their welfare, and would see with much concern and displeasure any acts of violence or oppression committed against them; that moreover, there are dwelling among those tribes many liberated Africans and British-born subjects whom Her Majesty's Government are bound to protect from injury. . . .

Proclamation

One might change the nature of imperial control and thus alter the machinery of government by proclamation. After the Sepoy mutiny —about which Alexander Duff wrote—had been suppressed in India, the East India Company was replaced by the British government. In 1858 Queen Victoria extended Crown rule over the company's former territories, by virtue of the following proclamation read in Allahabad on November first.

From *The Annual Register ... 1858* (London, 1859), I, 258–59.

We hereby announce to the native princes of India that all treaties and engagements made with them by or under the authority of the Hon. East India Company are by us accepted, and will be scrupulously maintained; and we look for the like observance on their part.

We desire no extension of our present territorial possessions: and while we will permit no aggression upon our dominions or our rights to be attempted with impunity, we shall sanction no encroachment on those of others. We shall respect the rights, dignity, and honour of native princes as our own; and we desire that they, as well as our own subjects, should enjoy that prosperity and that social advancement which can only be secured by internal peace and good government.

We hold ourselves bound to the natives of our Indian territories by the same obligations of duty which bind us to all our other subjects; and those obligations, by the blessing of Almighty God, we shall faithfully and conscientiously fulfil.

Firmly relying ourselves on the truth of Christianity, and acknowledging with gratitude the solace of religion, we disclaim alike the right and the desire to impose our convictions on any of our subjects. We declare it to be our Royal will and pleasure that none be in anywise favoured, none molested or disquieted by reason of their religious faith or observances, but that all shall alike enjoy the equal and impartial protection of the law; and we do strictly charge and enjoin all those who may be in authority under us that they abstain from all interference with the religious belief or worship of any of our subjects, on pain of our highest displeasure.

And it is our further will that, so far as may be, our subjects, of whatever race or creed, be freely and impartially admitted to offices in our service, the duties of which they may be qualified, by their education, ability, and integrity duly to discharge.

We know and respect the feelings of attachment with which the natives of India regard the lands inherited by them from their ancestors, and we desire to protect them in all rights connected therewith, subject to the equitable demands of the State, and we will that generally, in framing and administering the law, due regard be paid to the ancient rights, usages, and customs of India.

We deeply lament the evils and misery which have been brought upon India by the acts of ambitious men, who have deceived their countrymen by false reports and led them into open rebellion. Our power having been shown by the suppression of that rebellion in the field, we desire to show our mercy by pardoning the offences of those who have been thus misled, but who desire to return to the path of duty. . . .

Our clemency will be extended to all offenders, save and except those who have been or shall be convicted of having directly taken part in the murder of British subjects. With regard to such the demands of justice forbid the exercise of mercy. . . .

When, by the blessing of Providence, internal tranquillity shall be restored, it is our earnest desire to stimulate the peaceful industry of India, to promote works of public utility and improvement, and to administer its government for the benefit of all our subjects resident therein. In their prosperity will be our strength, in their contentment our security, and in their gratitude our best reward. And may the God of all power grant to us, and to those in authority under us, strength to carry out these our wishes for the good of our people.

Parliamentary Sovereignty

To guard against the possibility that a colony of settlement might enact legislation that was repugnant to British common law, the imperial Parliament passed, in 1865, the Colonial Laws Validity Act. While this act arose from specific conditions existing in the colony of South Australia, its application was sweeping. It was repealed for the Dominions (then Canada, Australia, New Zealand, South Africa, and Newfoundland) in 1931.

The entire act, with useful footnotes, may most conveniently be consulted in *Imperial Constitutional Documents, 1765–1952: A Supplement,* ed. Frederick Madden (Oxford: Basil Blackwell & Mott, 1953), pp. 67–70.

Whereas doubts have been entertained respecting the validity of divers laws enacted, or purporting to be enacted, by the Legislatures of certain of Her Majesty's colonies, and respecting the powers of such Legislatures; and it is expedient that such doubts should be removed: Be it hereby enacted. . . .

I. The term "Colony" shall in this Act include all of Her Majesty's possessions abroad, in which there shall exist a Legislature as hereinafter defined, except the Channel Islands, the Isle of Man, and such territories as may for the time being be vested in Her Majesty, under or by virtue of any Act of Parliament for the government of India:

The terms "Legislature" and "Colonial Legislature" shall severally signify the authority, other than the Imperial Parliament or Her Majesty in Council, competent to make laws for any colony:

The term "Representative Legislature" shall signify any colonial Legislature which shall comprise a legislative body of which one-half are elected by inhabitants of the colony:

The term "Colonial Law" shall include laws made for any colony, either by such Legislature as aforesaid or by Her Majesty in Council:

An Act of Parliament, or any provision thereof, shall in construing this Act, be said to extend to any colony when it is made applicable to such colony by the express words or necessary intendment of any Act of Parliament:

The term "Governor" shall mean the officer lawfully administering the Government of any colony:

The term "Letters Patent" shall mean Letters Patent under the Great Seal of the United Kingdom of Great Britain and Ireland.

II. Any colonial law, which is or shall be in any respect repugnant to the provisions of any Act of Parliament extending to the colony to which such law may relate, or repugnant to any order or regulation made under authority of such Act of Parliament, or having in the colony the force and effect of such Act, shall be read subject to such Act, order, or regulation, and shall, to the extent of such repugnancy, but not otherwise, be and remain absolutely void and inoperative.

III. No colonial law shall be, or be deemed to have been, void or inoperative on the ground of repugnancy to the law of England, unless the same shall be repugnant to the provisions of some such Act of Parliament, order, or regulation, as aforesaid.

IV. No colonial law, passed with the concurrence of, or assented to by the Governor of any colony, or to be hereafter so passed or assented to, shall be, or be deemed to have been, void or inoperative by reason only of any Instructions with reference to such law, or the subject thereof, which may have been given to such Governor, by or on behalf of Her Majesty, by any Instrument other than the Letters Patent or Instrument authorizing such Governor to concur in passing or to assent to laws for the peace, order, and good government of such colony, even though such Instructions may be referred to in such Letters Patent, or last-mentioned Instrument.

V. Every colonial Legislature shall have, and be deemed at all times to have had, full power within its jurisdiction to establish courts of judicature, and to abolish and reconstitute the same, and to alter the constitution thereof, and to make provision for the administration of justice therein; and every Representative Legislature shall, in respect to the colony under its jurisdiction have, and be deemed at all times to have had, full power to make laws respecting the constitution, powers, and procedure of such Legislature; provided that such laws shall have been passed in such manner and form as may from time to time be required, by any Act of Parliament, Letters Patent, Order in Council, or colonial law for the time being in force in the said colony.

VI. The certificate of the clerk or other proper officer of a legislative body in any colony to the effect that the document to which it is attached is a true copy of any colonial law assented to by the Governor of such colony, or of any bill reserved for the signification of Her Majesty's pleasure by the said Governor, shall be *prima facie* evidence that the document so certified is a true copy of such law or bill, and, as the case may be, that such law has been duly and properly passed and assented to, or that such bill has been duly and properly passed and presented to the Governor; and any proclamation purporting to be published by authority of the Governor, in any newspaper in the colony to which such law or bill shall relate, and signifying Her Majesty's disallowance of any such colonial law, or Her Majesty's assent to any such reserved bill as aforesaid, shall be *prima facie* evidence of such disallowance or assent.

Defense Agreements

An informal empire, far larger and certainly as important as the formal one, developed throughout the nineteenth and early twentieth centuries. Governments found that annexation was expensive, for with annexation came responsibilities for administration, education, sanitation, and transportation, all costing more than a colony might be worth, at least as measured in financial terms. An alternate means by which imperial sway might be extended was through agreements, or treaties, under which a European nation would guarantee the neutrality, territorial integrity, or defense of a nominally independent people. This was the case in China, as the American Open Door notes illustrated at the turn of the century, and in Brazil, Argentina, and Uruguay. It also was the case in Afghanistan, where, in July of 1880, the Sirdar Abdul Rahman Khan was recognized as Amir of Kabul and was given British protection.

From the Cabinet Papers, as quoted in *The Reluctant Imperialists: British Foreign Policy, 1878–1902*, ed. C. J. Lowe (London: Routledge & Kegan Paul Ltd., 1967), II, *The Documents*, 32. Crown-copyright; the original document is in the Public Record Office, London.

His Excellency the Viceroy and Governor General in Council has learnt with pleasure that your Highness has proceeded toward Kabul, in accordance with the invitation of the British Government. Therefore, in consideration of the friendly sentiments by which your Highness is animated, and of the advantage to be derived by the Sirdars and people from the establishment of a settled government under your Highness' authority, the British Government recognizes your Highness as Amir of Kabul.

I am furthered empowered, on the part of the Viceroy and Governor General of India, to inform your Highness that the British Government has no desire to interfere in the internal government of the territories in the possession of your Highness, and has no wish that an English Resident should be stationed anywhere within those territories. For the convenience of ordinary friendly intercourse, such as is maintained between two adjoining states, it may be advisable that a Muhammedan Agent of the British Government should reside, by agreement, at Kabul.

Your Highness has requested that the views and intentions of the British Government with regard to the position of the ruler of Kabul in relation to foreign powers, should be placed on record for your Highness' information. The Viceroy and Governor General in Council authorizes me to declare to you that since the British Government admits no right of interference by foreign powers within Afghanistan, and since both Russia and Persia are pledged to abstain from all interference with the affairs of Afghanistan, it is plain that your Highness can have no political relations with any foreign power except with the British Government. If any foreign power should attempt to interfere in Afghanistan, and if such interference should lead to unprovoked aggression on the dominions of your Highness, in that event the British Government would be prepared to aid you, to such extent and in such manner as may appear to the British Government necessary, in repelling it; provided that your Highness follows unreservedly the advice of the British Government in regard to your external relations.

International Convention

Frequently more than one European nation would have an interest in the trade opportunities of a particular area. This was especially true in Africa, after the forward thrust of the so-called new imperialism turned into a post-1874 scramble for colonies throughout the world. Prince Otto von Bismarck invited interested powers to meet in Berlin in November, 1884, in order to agree upon solutions to a number of problems which had arisen over the Congo and the Niger river basins. By the following February the signatories had agreed upon a General Act. Under its better known title, the Berlin Act, the agreement was meant to regulate European relations with major portions of west and central Africa. The most important articles from the act follow.

From *The Imperialism Reader: Documents and Readings on Modern Expansionism,* ed. Louis L. Snyder (Princeton: D. Van Nostrand Co., 1962), pp. 210–11.

Freedom of Trade to All Nations

Article I. The trade of all nations shall enjoy complete freedom. . . .

Article III. Wares, of whatever origin, imported into these regions, under whatsoever flag, by sea or river, or overland, shall be subject to no other taxes than such as may be levied as fair compensation for expenditure in the interests of trade, and which for this reason must be equally borne by the subjects themselves and by foreigners of all nationalities. . . .

Article IV. Merchandise imported into these regions shall remain free from import and transit dues. . . .

Article VI. All the powers exercising sovereign rights or influence in the aforesaid territories bind themselves to watch over the preservation of the native tribes, and to care for the improvement of the conditions of their moral and material well-being, and to help in suppressing slavery, and especially the slave trade. . . .

They shall, without distinction of creed or nation, protect and favour all religious, scientific, or charitable institutions, and undertakings created and organized for the above ends, or which aim at instructing the natives and bringing home to them the blessings of civilization. . . .

Christian missionaries, scientists, and explorers, with their followers, property, and collections, shall likewise be the objects of especial protection. . . .

Freedom of conscience and religious toleration are expressly guaranteed to the natives, no less than to subjects and to foreigners. . . .

The free and public exercise of all forms of Divine worship, and the right to build edifices for religious purposes, and to organize religious missions belonging to all creeds, shall not be limited or fettered in any way whatsoever. . . .

Article IX. Seeing that trading in slaves is forbidden in conformity with the principles of international law as recognized by the Signatory Powers, and seeing also that the operations, which, by sea or land, furnish slaves to trade, ought likewise to be regarded as forbidden, the Powers which do or shall exercise sovereign rights or influence in the territories forming the Conventional basin of the Congo declare that these territories may not serve as a market or means of transit for the trade in slaves, of whatever race they may be. Each of the Powers binds itself to employ all means at its disposal for putting an end to this trade and for punishing those who engage in it. . . .

Article XXXIV. Any power which henceforth takes possession of a tract of land on the coasts of the African continent outside of its present possessions, or which, hitherto without such possessions, shall acquire them, as well as the Power which assumes a Protectorate there, shall accompany the respective act with a notification thereof, addressed to the other Signatory Powers of the present Act, in order to enable them, if need be, to make good any claims of their own. . . .

Article XXXV. The Signatory Powers of the present Act recognize the obligation to insure the establishment of authority in regions occupied by them on the coasts of the African continent sufficient to protect existing rights, and, as the case may be, freedom of trade and of transit under the conditions agreed upon.

Concessions

Mineral and trading concessions often were obtained from tribal chiefs in exchange for arms and ammunition or other aid against tribal enemies. One of the most important concessions was won by Cecil John Rhodes, the English entrepreneur who sought to link the Cape of Good Hope to Cairo and paint all of east and south-central Africa red on the imperial map. In 1888 he sent three of his agents to negotiate a mineral grant from Lobengula, the king of Matabeleland and nearby areas. Upon obtaining the concession, Rhodes established the British South Africa Company, and the document ultimately was sold for shares in the chartered company to the value of £1,000,000.

From *The Life of the Rt. Hon. Cecil John Rhodes, 1853–1902,* 2 vols., by Sir Lewis Mitchell (London: Edward Arnold Ltd., 1910), I, 244–45. Reprinted by permission of A. P. Watt & Son.

Know all men by these presents, that whereas Charles Dunell Rudd, of Kimberley; Rochfort Maguire, of London; and Francis Robert Thompson,[1] of Kimberley, hereinafter called the grantees, have covenanted and agreed, and do hereby covenant and agree, to pay to me, my heirs and successors, the sum of one hundred pounds sterling, British currency, on the first day of every lunar month; and, further, to deliver at my royal kraal one thousand Martini-Henry breech-loading rifles, together with one hundred thousand rounds of suitable ball cartridge, five hundred of the said rifles and fifty thousand of the said cartridges to be ordered from England forthwith and delivered with reasonable despatch, and the remainder of the said rifles and cartridges to be delivered as soon as the said grantees shall have commenced to work mining machinery within my territory; and further, to deliver on the Zambesi River a steamboat with guns suitable for defensive purposes upon the said river, or in lieu of the said steamboat, should I so elect, to pay to me the sum of five hundred pounds sterling, British currency. On the execution of these presents, I, Lo Bengula, King of Matabeleland, Mashonaland, and other adjoining territories, in exercise of my sovereign powers, and in the presence and with the consent of my council of indunas, do hereby grant and assign unto the said grantees, their heirs, representatives, and assigns, jointly and severally, the complete and exclusive charge over all metals and minerals situated and contained in my kingdoms, principalities, and

[1] [Rudd had been Rhodes's partner in the diamond fields of South Africa, Maguire was a college friend, and Thompson was a local authority on Lobengula and Matabeleland.]

dominions, together with full power to do all things that they may deem necessary to win and procure the same, and to hold, collect, and enjoy the profits and revenues, if any, derivable from the said metals and minerals, subject to the aforesaid payment; and whereas I have been much molested of late by divers persons seeking and desiring to obtain grants and concessions of land and mining rights in my territories, I do hereby authorise the said grantees, their heirs, representatives, and assigns, to take all necessary and lawful steps to exclude from my kingdom, principalities, and dominions all persons seeking land, metals, minerals, or mining rights therein, and I do hereby undertake to render them all such needful assistance as they may from time to time require for the exclusion of such persons, and to grant no concessions of land or mining rights from and after this date without their consent and concurrence; provided that, if at any time the said monthly payment of one hundred pounds shall be in arrear for a period of three months, then this grant shall cease and determine from the date of the last-made payment; and, further, provided, that nothing contained in these presents shall extend to or affect a grant made by me of certain mining rights in a portion of my territory south of the Ramaquaban River, which grant is commonly known as the Tati Concession.

This, given under my hand this thirtieth day of October, in the year of our Lord 1888, at my royal kraal.

	[Lo Bengula] X [his mark].
Witness: Chas. D. Helm.	C. D. Rudd.
J. F. Dreyer.	Rochfort Maguire.
	F. R. Thompson.

Secret Agreements

Diplomacy had been conducted in secret during the Renaissance, and it continued to be shrouded in secrecy into the twentieth century. Covenants openly arrived at were the exception rather than the norm. When secret agreements involved two European powers only and were limited to mutual defense arrangements, there often were good reasons why they should be kept from public view. When the agreements were between European nations but involved non-European peoples, who were not consulted, it was imperative that they be kept secret.

During World War I, the British sought to encourage revolt in the Arab portions of the Ottoman Empire. The Turks, allied with the Central Powers against Britain and her associates, controlled the Near East; if Arab nationalism could be turned against the Ottomans, not only would an enemy nation be seriously distracted, but Britain and France might acquire new holdings. Sir Mark Sykes and Charles François Georges-Picot worked out an agreement by which Mesopotamia—present-day Iraq—and Syria would be split between their respective nations on an east-west axis. Russia agreed to share in the secret Sykes-Picot agreement in exchange for British and French approval of her claim to portions of Anatolia. In October, 1916, this tripartite agreement was reached through an exchange of letters. The most important of these had been written in May by the British Foreign Minister, Sir Edward Grey, to France's ambassador to the Court of St. James's, Paul Cambon.

From *Documents on British Foreign Policy, 1919–1939*, 15 vols., ed. Sir Ernest Llewellyn Woodward and Rohan Butler (London, 1952), IV, 245–47.

I have the honour to inform your Excellency . . . that the acceptance of the whole project, as it now stands, will involve the abdication of considerable British interests, but, since His Majesty's Government recognize the advantage to the general cause of the Allies entailed in producing a more favourable internal political situation in Turkey, they are ready to accept the arrangement now arrived at, provided that the co-operation of the Arabs is secured, and that the Arabs fulfil the conditions and obtain the towns of Homs, Hama, Damascus, and Aleppo.

It is accordingly understood between the French and British Governments—

1. That France and Great Britain are prepared to recognize and protect an independent Arab State or a Confederation of Arab States in the areas (A) and (B) marked on the annexed map [which

accompanied the letter] under the suzerainty of an Arab chief. That in area (A) France, and in area (B) Great Britain, shall have priority of right of enterprise and local loans. That in area (A) France, and in area (B) Great Britain, shall alone supply advisers of foreign functionaries at the request of the Arab State or Confederation of Arab States.

2. That in the blue area France, and in the red area Great Britain, shall be allowed to establish such direct or indirect administration or control as they desire and as they may think fit to arrange with the Arab State or Confederation of Arab States.

3. That in the brown area there shall be established an international administration, the form of which is to be decided upon after consultation with Russia, and subsequently in consultation with the other Allies, and the representatives of the Shereef of Mecca.

4. That Great Britain be accorded (1) the ports of Haifa and Acre, (2) guarantee of a given supply of water from the Tigris and Euphrates in area (A) for area (B). His Majesty's Government, on their part, undertake that they will at no time enter into negotiations for the cession of Cyprus to any third Power without the previous consent of the French Government.

5. That Alexandretta shall be a free port as regards the trade of the British Empire, and that there shall be no discrimination in port charges or facilities as regards British shipping and British goods; that there shall be freedom of transit for British goods through Alexandretta and by railway through the blue area, whether those goods are intended for or originate in the red area, or (B) area, or area (A); and there shall be no discrimination, direct or indirect, against British goods on any railway or against British goods or ships at any port serving the areas mentioned.

That Haifa shall be a free port as regards the trade of France, her dominions and protectorates, and there shall be no discrimination in port charges or facilities as regards French shipping and French goods. There shall be freedom of transit for French goods through Haifa and by the British railway through the brown area, whether those goods are intended for or originate in the blue area, area (A), or area (B), and there shall be no discrimination, direct or indirect, against French goods on any railway, or against French goods or ships at any port serving the areas mentioned.

6. That in area (A) the Bagdad Railway shall not be extended southwards beyond Mosul, and in area (B) northwards beyond Samarra, until a railway connecting Bagdad with Aleppo via the Euphrates Valley has been completed, and then only with the concurrence of the two Governments.

7. That Great Britain has the right to build, administer, and be sole owner of a railway connecting Haifa with area (B), and shall

have a perpetual right to transport troops along such a line at all times.

It is to be understood by both Governments that this railway is to facilitate the connexion of Bagdad with Haifa by rail. . . .

8. For a period of twenty years the existing Turkish customs tariff shall remain in force throughout the whole of the blue and red areas, as well as in areas (A) and (B), and no increase in the rates of duty or conversion from *ad valorem* to specific rates shall be made except by agreement between the two powers.

There shall be no interior customs barriers between any of the above-mentioned areas. The customs duties leviable on goods destined for the interior shall be collected at the port of entry and handed over to the administration of the area of destination.

9. It shall be agreed that the French Government will at no time enter into any negotiations for the cession of their rights and will not cede such rights in the blue area to any third Power, except the Arab State or Confederation of Arab States, without the previous agreement of His Majesty's Government, who, on their part, will give a similar undertaking to the French Government regarding the red area.

10. The British and French Governments . . . shall agree that they will not themselves acquire and will not consent to a third Power acquiring territorial possessions in the Arabian peninsula, nor consent to a third Power installing a naval base either on the east coast, or on the islands, of the Red Sea. This, however, shall not prevent such adjustment of the Aden frontier as may be necessary in consequence of recent Turkish aggression.

11. The negotiations with the Arabs as to the boundaries of the Arab State or Confederation of Arab States shall be continued through the same channel as heretofore on behalf of the two Powers.

12. It is agreed that measures to control the importation of arms into the Arab territories will be considered by the two Governments.

I have further the honour to state that, in order to make the agreement complete, His Majesty's Government are proposing to the Russian Government to exchange notes analogous to those exchanged by the latter and your Excellency's Government on the 26th April last. Copies of these notes will be communicated to your Excellency as soon as exchanged.

I would also venture to remind your Excellency that the conclusion of the present agreement raises, for practical consideration, the question of the claims of Italy to a share in any partition or rearrangement of Turkey in Asia, as formulated in article 9 of the agreement of the 26th April, 1915, between Italy and the Allies.

His Majesty's Government further consider that the Japanese Government should be informed of the arrangements now concluded. . . .

Trusteeship

A nation might also add to its holdings by simple conquest, by the pacification of native tribes, or through the spoils of war. In this way Britain acquired authority in vast portions of southern Africa, in Malaya, and in India, while Germany and France pressed forward against local groups in Indochina and east Africa. Britain acquired the major portions of the former German empire in 1919 as mandated territories. This arrangement was described in the context of a dual mandate in Africa by the man most responsible for the furthering of indirect rule on that continent, the former captain who was now Lord Lugard. Lugard was, very possibly, Belloc's William Blood.

From *The Dual Mandate in British Tropical Africa*, fourth edition, by Frederick Dealtry (later Lord) Lugard (Edinburgh: William Blackwood & Sons, Ltd., 1929), pp. 50–59. Reprinted by permission of the publisher.

The principles which should guide the controlling Powers in Africa were first laid down with international sanction in the Berlin Act of 1885, which . . . "aimed at the extension of the benefits of civilisation to the natives, the promotion of trade and navigation on the basis of perfect equality for all nations, and the preservation of the territories affected from the ravages of war." The moral obligations towards the natives were dealt with more explicitly and amplified by the Brussels Act, which came into operation in 1892, and have lately received a wider and more practical sanction under the Treaty of Versailles and the Convention of September 1919. . . .

. . . Article 22 embodies the latest expression of the conscience of Europe in regard to "peoples not yet able to stand by themselves," and constitutes not only a pledge in respect of Mandate territories, but a model and an aspiration for the conduct of those already under the control of one or other of the signatories. . . . There was, however, much unfortunate delay detrimental to the welfare of the countries concerned in issuing the Mandates. This was due in part to the difficulty of harmonising the views of the Mandatories, and in part to the claim of the United States to be consulted as to their terms.

The Mandates were conferred by the Supreme Council of the victorious Allies, and, after acceptance by each Mandatory, were submitted to the Council of the League of Nations, which was charged with the duty of seeing that their terms were in accordance with the Covenant. Thereafter the Powers which had accepted them became "Mandatories of the League," to which they must submit an annual report. A permanent Commission was set up consisting of nine members appointed by the Council, the majority being nationals of non-Mandatory Powers. They are selected "for personal merit and competence," as private individuals holding no office under their Governments, and in no way representative of their nations. Their duty is to examine the annual reports in the presence of the representative of the Mandatory in order to see that the conditions of the Mandate are being observed, and to report to the Council, which alone communicates with the Powers.

The Mandates were of three types: *Class A.* includes the ex-Turkish colonies—Iraq, Palestine, and Syria,—whose independence "can be provisionally recognised subject to the rendering of administrative advice and assistance" until they are able to stand alone. Their wishes must be a principal consideration in the selection of the Mandatory. *Class B.* comprises the Central African ex-German colonies. The Mandatory in this case is responsible for the administration, and undertakes to maintain public order and to promote the moral and material welfare of the people. *Class C.* includes South-West Africa and the Pacific Islands. Here the Mandatory administers the territory under its own laws as an integral portion of its own territory, subject to the safeguards named for the interests of the natives.

The essential conditions and obligations in respect of Classes *B.* and *C.* are: (1) freedom of conscience and religion, subject only to the maintenance of public order and morals; (2) prohibition of abuses, such as the arms and liquor traffic and the slave trade; (3) prevention of fortifications, military and naval bases, or the military training of natives except for police and defence; and (in Class *B.*) equal commercial opportunity for all members of the League. "It is not in the power of the Council of the League or of the principal Powers to alter these. Amendments can only be made if the Covenant is revised."

In the *A.* Class Great Britain holds Mandates for Iraq and Palestine. In the *B.* Class for less than one-sixth of the Cameruns, for nearly a third of Togo, and for the greater part of German East Africa (Tanganyika). In the *C.* Class she holds no Mandate, but those granted to the Union of South Africa for "German South-West Africa," to Australia for New Guinea and other Pacific islands south of the Equator, to New Zealand for Samoa, and to the British Empire for Nauru are all conferred upon the King "on behalf of" the various Mandatories.

The Mandate system was an attempt to compose conflicting claims, pledges, and ideals. The Allies have loudly condemned the colonial methods of Germany and Turkey. Led by President [Woodrow] Wilson, they had given currency to the catchwords "No Annexations," "Self-determination," and "The Open Door," and stood committed to the principles they implied. They sought, moreover, for a method which should remedy the defects of the Berlin and Brussels Acts by providing something in the way of a supervising authority to ensure the observance of the pledges given. The alternatives were annexation, or joint international administration, which would assuredly give rise to friction, would paralyse all initiative and progress by the dead hand of a super-bureaucracy devoid of national sentiment and stifling to all patriotism, and would be very disadvantageous to the countries concerned. Since this was admittedly impracticable, annexation was strongly advocated by the Japanese and the three Dominion Governments. It was, however, opposed to the principles proclaimed by the Allies, if not in some cases, to definite pre-Armistice pledges. A compromise was with difficulty reached by dividing the Mandates into the three classes described. The C. Mandates held by Japan and the Dominions "amount," as General [Jan Christian] Smuts observed, "to annexation in all but the name,"—save for the obligations imposed in regard to the natives, and the annual report to the League.

The Mandate system is a new departure in international law and policy, in that it confers sovereignty under definite obligations, for the fulfilment of which the Mandatory is responsible to a constituted authority. Its closest analogies were the Mandate conferred on King Leopold of Belgium as sovereign of the Congo State—which, however, lacked a clear definition of the obligations and a supervising body,—and the proposal made by President [Theodore] Roosevelt in 1906 that France and Spain should hold a joint "Mandate" for Morocco, and that they should render to Italy, as the supervising authority on behalf of all the Powers, with the right of inspection and verification, a complete report, so as to ensure that the claims of Germany and the United States to equal commercial opportunity were duly observed. Though probably the best solution of a question which at the moment threatened to produce very serious difficulties, it is naturally open to criticisms, some of which may be briefly noted.

1. The Covenant lays down as regards the A. class of Mandates that "the wishes of the communities must be a principal consideration in the selection of the Mandatory." It is asserted that the Powers by the neglect of this proviso have disregarded a fundamental injunction of the Covenant. The paragraphs of Article 22, upon which the B. and C. Mandates are based, contain no similar injunction. These territories have been divided up in most cases as best suited the jealousies of the Powers, sometimes with scanty regard even to tribal boundaries. Great Britain and France even undertook to compensate Italy by cession of territory if they increased their possessions in Africa as a consequence of the war. It is to be hoped that this is the last occasion on which the conscience of Europe will permit the exchange of "possessions" in Africa, as though they and their inhabitants were mere chattels for barter regardless of the pledges of protection,

for the fulfilment of which the protecting Power is individually responsible, and which it has no moral right to transfer to another. It is a notable proof of the one-sided character of the so-called treaties.

2. The Mandate to France for Togo and the Cameruns differs in one respect from the British Mandate for those countries, in that it appears to permit the recruitment of troops for service in emergency outside the territory. It seems difficult to reconcile this clause with the terms of Article 22.

3. Though the Allies professed to proclaim the doctrine of "equal commercial opportunity," there is no stipulation to this effect in the paragraphs of Article 22, on which the *A*. and *C*. Mandates are based. In the former, it is true that the principle is affirmed in the Mandates themselves, but, as in the *B*. class, it is restricted to members of the League, to the exclusion apparently of the United States and Germany. . . .

4. A serious drawback of the Mandate system lies at present in the fact that it constitutes only [a precarious title]. . . . The Mandatory, therefore, may be unwilling to expend large sums in economic development, and is only able to grant a conditional title or to enter into conditional contracts with any private firm which may be anxious to invest capital in the development of the country. Business men will not risk their capital when (*a*) the Mandate is (theoretically at least) revocable; (*b*) the Mandatory may at any time resign the Mandate without the loss of national prestige which would be involved if it were a part of the national possessions; (*c*) the Mandatory may prematurely consider that the country is ripe for self-government, and may transfer control to a native authority unable or unwilling to grant adequate protection. This is manifestly a serious drawback to the material progress of a mandated territory, and it is essential that some form of guarantee by the League or the Mandatory should be given. Failing this, annexation, if conditioned by all the existing safeguards, would probably find many advocates.

5. The question of the national status of the inhabitants of a Mandated territory has recently been the subject of exhaustive examination by the Mandates Commission and the Council of the League. . . . It is proposed that the inhabitants shall have the status of "persons administered or protected under Mandate." This would appear to be merely descriptive of their condition, and a definition of the rights connoted by the term is desirable. Though the legal status of a "protected person" in a British protectorate may be vague, his condition . . . differs little in practice from that of the inhabitant of a colony. He has no divided or precarious allegiance. His loyalty and patriotism (which count for much in Africa) are enlisted on behalf of the suzerain Power. But the person "protected under Mandate" shares with the owner of an estate "un titre précaire" subject to the con-

tingencies of revocation, rendition, or resignation of the Mandate, and has no definitely legalised status and rights. . . .

Some of these difficulties can, it would seem, only be solved by annexation, or at least by the declaration of a protectorate by the present Mandatories. On the assumption that there is no intention of ever restoring these countries to their former rulers, the principal objection to such a course seems to be one of sentiment, *provided that the annexing Powers accept as a condition of annexation all the conditions imposed by the present Mandates (including the annual report to the League) in the form of an international Convention.* . . .

. . . The great principle of trusteeship for backward races, though limited in its context to ex-enemy colonies, must obviously in future be regarded as no less applicable to the "possessions" of the Allies. The camouflage . . . is swept away, and the Powers, instead of arguing over the theoretical basis of sovereignty in Africa, frankly recognise that "the tutelage of nations not yet able to stand by themselves must be intrusted to advanced nations." They accept control under the Covenant primarily in the interests of the subject races.

The responsibility is one which the advantages of an inherited civilisation and a superior intellectual culture, no less than the physical superiority conferred by the monopoly of firearms, imposes upon the controlling Power. To the backward races civilisation must be made to mean something higher than the aims and methods of the development syndicate or the assiduous cultivation of new wants. Where these principles have been neglected, history has taught us that failure has been the result.

Such have been the successive steps by which Europe has sought to fulfil the Dual Mandate in Africa. . . . The moral obligations to the subject races include such matters as the training of native rulers; the delegation to them of such responsibility as they are fit to exercise; the constitutions of Courts of Justice free from corruption and accessible to all; the adoption of a system of education which will assist progress without creating false ideals; the institution of free labour and of a just system of taxation; the protection of the peasantry from oppression, and the preservation of their rights in land, &c.

The material obligations, on the other hand, are concerned with development of natural resources for the mutual benefit of the people and of mankind in general. They involve the examination of such questions as "equal opportunity" and "Imperial Preference," and other problems of economic policy. . . .

Nor is the obligation which the controlling Powers owe to themselves and their race a lesser one. It has been well said that a nation, like an individual, must have some task higher than the pursuit of material gain, if it is to escape the benumbing influence of parochialism and to fulfil its higher destiny. If high standards are maintained, the control of subject races must have an effect on national character which is not measurable in terms of material profit and loss. And what is true for the nation is equally true for the individual officers employed. If lower standards are adopted—the arrogant display of power, or the selfish pursuit of profit—the result is equally fatal to the nation and to the individual. Misuse of opportunity carries with it a relentless Nemesis, deteriorating the moral fibre of the individual, and permeating the nation. . . .

But if the standard which the white man must set before him when dealing with uncivilised races must be a high one for the sake of his own moral and spiritual balance, it is not less imperative for the sake of the influence which he exercises upon those over whom he is set in authority. The white man's prestige must stand high when a few score are responsible for the control and guidance of millions. His courage must be undoubted, his word and pledge absolutely inviolate, his sincerity transparent. There is no room for "mean whites" in tropical Africa. Nor is there room for those who, however high their motives, are content to place themselves on the same level as the uncivilised races. They lower the prestige by which alone the white races can hope to govern and to guide. . . .

Conquest

A nation might simply conquer another, acquire its territories and its native inhabitants by annexation, and administer them as part of those new empires that arose to replace the old. A dramatic example of the confrontation between imperialism arose late in 1941 when the Japanese invaded British-held Malaya. Considering themselves to be liberators of fellow Asians, as well as conquerors of Europeans, the Japanese moved with great speed down the Malay peninsula to attack the "fortress of Singapore" from the rear. There they accepted the surrender of eighty thousand British and Indian troops, in the single greatest military disaster the British Empire ever experienced. The Greater East Asia Co-Prosperity Sphere, the Japanese assumption of racial superiority over Europeans, and the ambivalent attitudes of many Malay leaders, who hoped for independence under neither European nor outside Asian auspices, provided mirror images to the earlier phases of European imperial expansion. The following selection comes from a translation of an eye-witness account of the fall of Singapore, written by Masanobu Tsuji, the Chief of Operations and Planning Staff for the Twenty-Fifth Japanese Army in Malaya.

From Colonel Masanobu Tsuji, *Singapore: The Japanese Version,* trans. by Margaret E. Lake, ed. by H. V. Howe (London, 1962), pp. 216–22. Published by Constable & Co. (London) and by Ure Smith Pty. Limited (Australia). Reprinted by permission of Laurence Pollinger Ltd. (authors' agents) and of Ure Smith.

Singapore was Britain's pivotal point in the domination of Asia. It was the eastern gate for the defence of India and the northern gate for the defence of Australia. It was the axis of the steamship route from Europe to the Orient, north to Hong Kong and through to Shanghai, and to the treasures of the Dutch East Indies to the south and east. Through these two arteries alone, during a period of many years, Britain controlled the Pacific Ocean with Singapore as the very heart of the area. . . .

Britain's boast that Singapore was an impregnable fortress, and her attempted coercion of Japan by dispatching to Singapore the two great and efficient battleships *Repulse* and *Prince of Wales,* were things that remain fresh even now in the memory of the people of Japan.

Singapore was naturally easy to defend, and with consolidation of its equipment could be shaped into an impregnable fortress. Facing the sea coast a battery of fifteen-inch guns was installed which dominated the eastern mouth of Johore Strait and protected the vast military barracks at Changi. The fortress was constructed in steel and concrete, and the world's greatest guns directed their forbidding muzzles towards the sea front. The military aerodromes of Tengah, Kallang, Seletar and Sembawang were good bases of operation for a large air force, and in Seletar naval harbour two great docks were installed which could easily take in fifty-thousand-ton battleships. . . .

In this great fortress, which Britain boasted could never be captured by attack from the sea, there was however an important weak point. . . . [T]he rear defences in the region of Johore Province were incomplete. This resulted from a defect in the organization of the fortress, or rather from a defect in the plan of military operations.

In other words, to land in southern Thailand, brave the intense heat and the long distance of eleven hundred kilometres, and advance through dense jungle, was probably deemed an impossibility by what seemed to the British common-sense judgment. A Japanese Army contemplating such operations in an emergency, would, it appeared, in view of the long distance overland, have to labour for perhaps more than a year to reach Singapore from Thailand. In the meantime it was not difficult to imagine that the British would complete fortification of the landward front.

In barely fifty-five days, however, the Japanese Army overwhelmed Malaya, carrying everything before it, and during the campaign the British, not being gods, were never certain of our whereabouts. . . .

Our estimate of the British defences and strength in Singapore was made on the basis of information that had been accumulated by all possible means. The five chief points were as follows:

1. Before the outbreak of hostilities it was estimated that the British forces in Malaya numbered from five to six brigades of regular troops, and two brigades of volunteers. Later, after examination of prisoners of war taken up to the end of January, this estimate was revised.

2. The enemy, relying on the strength of the fortress, would probably resist strongly, but owing to the fact that there were a tremendous number of non-combatants in Singapore, it was unlikely they would resist to the last man. With the addition of the refugees who had fled into the island during the hostilities on the mainland, the population of the island was considered to exceed one million. There were sufficient rations for the army for from one to two years, but there were not enough provisions to feed a population of one million for any length of time. This was a very serious weakness from the point of view of defence.

3. The pivotal point of the defences was the sea front only. After the commencement of hostilities rear defences were hurriedly constructed in about two months. They were well sited, and behind barbed-wire entanglements, but without permanent fortification they were little more formidable than ordinary field entrenchments. . . .

4. . . . Loss of the reservoir would be fatal.

5. The rise and fall of tide in Johore Strait is roughly two metres and the current flows fairly fast, but there was a possibility we would be able to use collapsible motor boats. Because of the presence of enemy gunboats and their remaining air force the crossing of the strait presented some difficulty, and it did not appear possible to exercise effective control of troops who survived the crossing. Fortunately, mechanical mines had not been laid in the strait, except at its mouth. The adoption by the enemy of "seafire" tactics (ignition of crude petroleum discharged on the surface of the water) was anticipated and counter-measures were taken. . . .

The enemy, exhausted and demoralized after their retreat from the mainland, had sought shelter in the fortress. We had to commence our attack without giving them even a day's respite to rest and reorganize and recover their morale. We knew accurately our own fighting power and the condition of the enemy, and had the whole island fortress under close observation. It was decided to issue the orders for assault without delay.

I finished writing the final plan for the reduction of Singapore by sitting up all night. It was approved by the Army Commander at Kluang Headquarters the following morning. On 1st February at 10 a.m., divisional commanders and senior officers numbering about forty were assembled in the Skudai rubber jungle, and to the rumble of the guns [Lieutenant-] General [Tomoyuki] Yamashita impressively issued the Army orders to those present. Reading in a clear voice his face was flushed, and on the cheeks of the men listening tears could be seen. The spirits of the seventeen hundred men killed in action since the landing at Singora were believed by all to be present at this meeting.

Each of us received, in the lid of a canteen, a little of the Imperial gift of *Kikumasumune* [wine], and we drank a toast: "It is a good place to die. Certainly we shall conquer."

Occupation

Where white settlers came to live, they often became the active force in maintaining the idea and conditions of imperialism, proving to be far more conservative than the Colonial power itself. A particularly striking instance of conflict arising over white settlement occurred in east Africa. After World War I white settlers there demanded self-government, especially in Kenya, which in 1920 became a Crown colony. In a revolutionary White Paper a commission chaired by the Duke of Devonshire proclaimed the doctrine of native paramountcy: "Kenya is an African territory." Where the interests of native and immigrant conflicted, the former were to prevail. But this principle, enunciated in 1923, was changed by two subsequent commissions— those of Ormsby-Gore in 1926, which emphasized a union of Kenya, Tanganyika, and Uganda, and of Hilton Young in 1929, which returned to the idea of trusteeship. One man who sought to testify before this commission, in vain, was a native, Johnstone Kenyatta. Afterward, taking the name of Jomo, he became secretary of the Kikuyu Central Association and, with Makhan Singh, a pro-African Indian trade unionist, began what would be a long history of Kenyan unrest. War intervened, and after World War II the white settlers of Kenya sought to return to pre-war conditions. The following extract from the *Kenya Settlement Handbook* for 1949 shows how little the Europeans had changed. In 1952 the colony was plunged into a state of emergency over the so-called Mau Mau terrorist campaigns, and eleven years later was an independent nation—with Jomo Kenyatta as its chief officer shortly thereafter.

From *The Kenya Settlement Handbook 1949* (Aylesbury, Eng., n.d.), pp. 91–94. Published by The Commissioner for European Settlement, Nairobi.

Kenya is by no means only a country for farmers, and is well known as an extremely attractive place in which to reside. Most districts have their clubs where golf, tennis, and, in some cases, polo, and squash rackets are available, whilst cricket, rugby, association football and hockey are played in the larger centres. The more sedentary social amenities are as readily obtainable in Kenya as in other countries.

Horses do well in most parts of the Highlands, and there are several packs which hunt jackal or buck. Racing is a most popular and inexpensive sport, and racecourses, with regular meetings, are to be found in several of the more important centres. The Pony Club for children is a flourishing institution. There is rough bird shooting, but big game shooting, with rifle or cine-camera, is a more plentiful sport. The fisherman, too, has ample opportunity, for well-stocked trout streams abound in the Colony. Good deep-sea fishing is to be found outside Mombasa. Yachting is still in its infancy, but there is good small boat racing at Mombasa on the coast, on Lake Naivasha in the midst of the Highlands, and at Kisumu on Lake Victoria.

For many years past, Mombasa island and many places along the mainland coast have been used as holiday resorts. There is good hotel accommodation both in Mombasa island and along the mainland coast, and private houses can be leased for house-parties. Bathing in comparatively smooth water is to be had in the lagoon behind the coral reef which extends, with only a few gaps, all along the coast, or surf bathing where the gaps are sufficiently wide to allow the rollers to come right in to the sandy beach. As already mentioned, there is excellent yacht racing round Mombasa island, whilst the more adventurous can cruise up and down the coast or go farther afield, for example, to Zanzibar. The north-east and south-east tradewinds which blow steadily, and alternate every six months, provide a never-failing motive power.

The climate of the Highlands . . . is an extremely pleasant one to live in. Gardening, particularly at the higher altitudes, is a joy to those so minded, and gardens can be made very attractive with the trees and the wide green lawns, and the shrubs and flowers of temperate climes. Even in the lower and drier districts there is a blaze of colour during the rainy seasons, and semi-tropical shrubs thrive.

All the necessities of life can now be readily obtained locally, and there is no need for individuals to import them for their personal use. The shops are well stocked with clothes and household goods, and tailoring establishments abound. Naturally, the larger towns are the best shopping centres, but immediate necessities can be got almost anywhere. All food is locally produced and is of good standard. Meat, fish, dairy, pig and poultry products are plentiful, as are all kinds of fresh vegetables and many kinds of fruit.

There are daily and weekly newspapers and a local broadcasting station. English and foreign short-wave radio stations are well received. Amateur theatricals are popular, but the cinema provides most of the evening entertainment, and there are good cinemas in Nairobi showing up-to-date pictures. Other townships are catered for, sometimes by travelling cinemas and in some cases by cinema theatres of their own. Travelling about the country can be done both by car and rail, the former being the more usual. Cars of British manufacture are readily obtainable and service garages abound everywhere. Nairobi, the capital, has a fleet of buses serving the residential areas on its outskirts.

Social and cultural amenities are steadily improving with the aid of such institutions as the McMillan and Carnegie Libraries, the Arts

and Crafts Society, the Natural History Society, the Coryndon
Museum and the Musical and Dramatic Societies.

The English, Scottish and Roman Catholic Churches and other
religious bodies are well represented and have commodious church
buildings in most centres.

As the attractions of Kenya have matured and become more widely
known, there has been a considerable increase of residential settlers
recruited from those whose life's work has been in the Colony and
those who have spent much of their lives elsewhere. Such settlement
has been either on residential plots of 5 to 20 acres near towns or on
residential farms of 50 acres and upwards in suitable country districts.
In the former case, the attraction is the shopping facilities and
amusements of the town, coupled with country life in its more gregar-
ious form. In the latter case, it is the spacious life which appeals, and
there is the opportunity and added interest of keeping a small dairy
herd and growing vegetables and fruit, so furnishing fresh food for
the table and a small surplus for sale. The opportunity to ride and
fish and to find country sports almost at the door is another great
attraction in this kind of settlement, and certain districts are well
suited for it. There is plenty of room for both types of residential
settlement in Kenya.

Respect

One could also expand imperial power by respecting native institutions and working within them. This the French did in major portions of their empire, and the British applied their concept of indirect rule in Malaya, Samoa, and selected areas of Africa. Respect implied more than ruling indirectly, however, and it paid greater dividends than relatively trouble-free administrations. The following Minute, written by Sir Hugh Clifford to the Lieutenant-Governor of the Northern Provinces of Nigeria in March of 1922, indicates the context in which the desirability of studying native thought was placed. Clifford had learned to respect the native and his way of life in his early posts in Perak, Pahang, and North Borneo (now Sabah). He had been Governor of the Gold Coast (now Ghana), was at the time he wrote this Minute Governor in Kaduna, and later became Governor of Ceylon and of the Straits Settlements.

This minute is in the Public Record Office in London. It is reprinted more fully, and with informative commentary, in A. H. M. Kirke-Greene, ed., *The Principles of Native Administration in Nigeria: Selected Documents, 1900–1947* (London: Oxford University Press, 1965), pp. 174–86.

Everywhere throughout this wide expanse of country . . . I found a profoundly peaceful, diligent, prosperous and thriving peasantry, tilling their fields in complete confidence and security, governed by their own hereditary rulers, and living under forms of government which are the natural growth of their own political genius, and which owe nothing to exotic systems that have no sanction in local custom and tradition. That an enormous change—a change almost incalculably great—has been effected, since the beginning of the present century, in the character of the Governments under which these millions of human beings live and move and have their being is, of course, a fact. The salient feature, however, of the system of administration which was inaugurated by Sir George Taubman Goldie in the days when the Niger Company exercised administrative functions, and which, during the past five and twenty years, has been gradually extended over the Northern Provinces, is that the change which has been wrought has entailed no abrupt violent departure from established custom or tradition, none save minor alterations in the administrative machinery which had been developed by the people centuries before our Protectorate over them was established; no material modification even in the laws under which they live, save only that the traffic in slaves is no longer sanctioned by them. The change, which is so great as to amount to an absolute transformation, affecting alike the social, material and many of the moral conditions amid which these people live, abides wholly in the manner in which the indigenous system of government is today being made to function, and in the wholly new spirit in which Emirs and their Chiefs and Officials, from the Waziri and Galadima to the smallest Village Head, are being gradually and patiently taught to discharge the responsibilities and to carry out the duties which devolve upon them under that system. . . .

It must be the aim of the efficient Political Officer attached to a Native Administration to steer a middle course between . . . two extremes. He should keep steadily before him, in the first place, the cardinal fact that all executive authority is vested, not in him, but in the Native Administration; and that his proper functions are primarily advisory and for the rest are supervisory. He must recognize from the outset that, in all transactions between himself and the ruling classes in the Mohammedan States, he is dealing with a proud, sensitive and timid people, and that the timidity to which they are a prey is due, not so much to moral cowardice, but to an instinctive shrinking from the embarrassment and humiliation that are produced by the impatience, the roughness of manner, the loss of temper, the discourtesy, or any apparent contempt of, or disregard for, their accepted usages and traditions which they may, from time to time, think that they detect in those whom they recognize as occupying positions of authority over them. This feeling of timidity and uneasiness is immeasurably enhanced if any doubt is felt as to the ability of a European officer completely to understand all that is said to him; or by a corresponding doubt upon their part as to how far they are interpreting accurately the orders or ideas which he is endeavouring to impart to them through the medium of the vernacular. . . .

The Political Officer must also keep well in the foreground of his mind the fact that the folk with whom he is dealing are, or believe themselves to be, quite pathetically impotent; that they very rarely believe themselves to be in a position to resent openly any affront that a European may put upon them, no matter whether it be the result of set intention, or the mere blunderings of ignorance and indifference. It is therefore incumbent upon the efficient Political Officer to adopt toward all Mohammedans of standing, whether they are or are not officials in the employment of a Native Administration, what I can only adequately describe as a certain chivalry of manner, treating them with a measure of dignity and courtesy corresponding as nearly as possible to that which usually inspires their own behaviour, and scrupulously avoiding violent gestures, loudness of speech, or even the unnecessary raising of the speaking voice when addressing them. It must be one of the primary objects of every Political Officer to inspire the Africans of all classes with whom he has to deal, not only with respect, but with confidence; and neither the one nor the other is to be won by the European whose faults of manner are calculated to convey to the natives about him the idea that he is either a hectoring bully, a mannerless oaf, or, it may be, merely a buffoon. Similarly, it is very rarely safe to venture upon anything resembling a humourous sally when talking to Mohammedans of the superior classes, unless the individual addressed is exceedingly well known to the speaker. No one could dream of denying to the Hausa or the Fulani the possession of a sense of humour; and, indeed, I make no doubt that this has not infrequently been employed to convulse delighted local audiences with admirably rendered accounts of interviews with the more experienced members of the Political Staff during which, at the time, the latter have flattered themselves that they had succeeded in creating no mean impression. The Mohammedan of the upper classes, however, usually reserves his quips and jests for his intimates, and he is apt to regard any departure from this rule by a European as undignified, or if, as not infrequently happens, the point of the pleasantry be missed, as something which is embarrassingly incomprehensible, or possibly even offensive.

Finally, Political Officers should make a painstaking study of the innumerable little details governing the everyday demeanour and comportment of the Mohammedans among whom they are living which, taken together, constitute in their eyes the difference between good and bad manners. Had this been done in Nigeria at an earlier stage by all the Europeans who came into the country, we should not today be so frequently treated to the deplorable spectacle of well-meaning Mohammedans throughout the whole Dependency baring their heads as an intended token of respect (which in their own eyes it can never be) when greeting or addressing Europeans. This study should be extended to the predilections and prejudices of the people; and wherever possible, these should be carefully and even scrupulously respected. To give a concrete instance of what I mean. Some Political Officers living among Mohammedans should never for an instant forget that, according to the teaching of the Mohammedan religion, the dog ranks next after the pig on the list of "unclean" animals; that physical contact with a dog, no matter how accidental, to an orthodox Mohammedan, is or should be, an unspeakable pollution; that he instinctively feels, not only repulsion but contempt, at the sight of a European fondling his pet dog; and that mere elementary courtesy and respect for one's neighbour's feelings, to say nothing of one's own self-respect, should restrain a Political Officer, whose duty brings him into close daily intercourse with cultured Mohammedans, from wantonly offending prejudices of this character. During a visit which was paid to me at a Residency in the Northern Provinces by one of the leading Fulani Emirs in September, 1919—

that is to say, within a very few weeks of my arrival in Nigeria,—I was horrified to see two or three dogs, the property of the Political Officer in whose house the meeting was taking place, being allowed to run at large in and out among the Mohammedan officials who had their seats upon carpets spread upon the floor. I at once interfered; but that such an incident could be *possible,* showed either gross ignorance of Mohammedan feelings and prejudices, or a no less gross callousness and indifference to them; and either the one or the other, and still more a combination of both, argue the possession of qualities which are of a character effectually to bar those sentiments of mutual respect and confidence without which it is not feasible for a European to establish really intimate and sympathetic relations with cultured Mohammedans.

To Your Honour and to many of the senior Political Officers in the Northern Provinces, all this may appear very rudimentary. My object in addressing to you this Minute, however, is to impress upon the very large number of young officers, who have recently joined the Political Service of the Northern Provinces, two elementary but essential facts—viz., the great importance of cultivated good manners in their dealings with Mohammedans of all classes; and the impossibility of achieving this without first undertaking a careful and sympathetic study of native ideas, standards of courtesy, prejudices and predilections.

Some young Englishmen newly arrived in the country, and even, it is to be feared, some Political Officers of much longer standing, may perhaps ask: "Why should I bother myself about what the natives think about me and my manners? Why should I be at pains to study their ideas and prejudices? If my way of comporting myself is good enough for me, it has got to be good enough for them." The answer is that, for every European, the shy confidence of a primitive Mohammedan people is hedged about by barriers as formidable as those which guarded the Palace of the Sleeping Beauty; and that if any attempt is to be made to scale or penetrate them, the initiative must come from the white man. Unless, therefore, he be prepared scrupulously to refrain from raising fresh and unnecessary barriers of his own creation—such as are so easily reared up by faults of manner and of taste, as such things are judged from the native standpoint—he must be content to abandon at the very outset of his career, what should be one of the main objects of his ambition. This in turn means that he must resign himself for all his official life to the fate of one who is groping his way about an imperfectly lighted room, filled with unfamiliar, puzzling and often singularly angular objects. He will be condemning himself to *guessing,* in circumstances in which sure and intimate *knowledge* should guide him by its clear light to absolute certainty: and his guessing will often be at fault. Yet upon his reading of a situation, and upon the advice that he may tender to Government may depend the difference between justice and injustice (as such things are judged by the natives concerned); the difference between the honour and the dishonour of the Government which he is serving; the difference between good, honest work accomplished, such as may be held to justify any man's existence, and a piece of slipshod, indifferent, fudged make-shift, the poor quality of which must be manifest even to its uncritical author. For really first-class political work in this country, it must be remembered, cannot be done by the light of nature, on the spur of occasion, or without long preliminary preparation. Knowledge, sure and unerring knowledge of the people, of their character, of their point of view, of their customs, traditions, habits, modes of thought, is needed as the solid foundation upon which alone really sound political work can be reared up; and this has to be garnered slowly, patiently, painfully, little by little. It is not to be acquired as occasion requires. It is the fruit of the labour of years: it can never come as the happy inspiration of the moment. . . .

. . . In the Northern Provinces of Nigeria today, men do not spend year after year in continuous isolation or pass month after month without seeing a white face or speaking a word of their own language, and the opportunities for acquiring a deep and intimate knowledge of the people among whom we are working are proportionately restricted. What I would seek to impress upon young men now entering the Service, however, is that the possession of that knowledge is today as vitally important to England, and to the tremendously responsible work which she has undertaken to do in her Tropical Possessions, as it was five and twenty years ago; that to every one of them a splendid opportunity is vouchsafed of learning more about the people among whom he is living than is known to the rank and file of his fellows; that here, ready to his hand, is one of the most fascinating studies upon which it is given to any man to have the supreme good fortune to embark,—a study which is not only compellingly engrossing in itself, but which is bound enormously to enhance the value of the student to the Government he is serving, and proportionately to enlarge his individual power for good and his ability to serve faithfully both England and the pathetically defenceless people, the control or management of whose affairs England has given to him in trust.

In a very peculiar degree, we Political Officers in these distant lands have the honour of our country in our keeping; and I should like to see every man in the Service realizing this to the full. . . . It is a cheap fashion of our time to mock at enthusiasm, to be rather shy of confessing to such a weakness as the possession of ideas, to be a little ashamed of appearing to be actuated by any save purely selfish and material motives. That is, however, in many cases, I am convinced, a mere surface pose that is often designed to hide far more serious sentiments and ambitions which, precisely because they are serious and deeply felt, are not easy of expression by the average Englishmen. . . .

. . . We should realize that while, as I have already pointed out, a Political Officer living among these people has an immense number of difficult things to learn, that which he has to *teach* must be imparted slowly, cautiously, and with the utmost patience, his every act and judgement being inspired by a thorough appreciation of the native, rather than of the European, point of view. It is his primary business to insure that life, liberty and property are safeguarded, and to prevent both the old customary powers of chiefs being abused, and new forms of extortion and oppression from becoming prevalent. To this end he should be ubiquitous, accessible at all hours to the meanest suitor, patient with a patience far exceeding that of the Patriarch, and at once firm and just in all his dealings, alike with the rulers and with the folk they rule. Yet throughout he should not judge the wrong-doer by standards not his own for it is quite easy through an over-zeal for justice, to be betrayed into acts that are unjust. This being so, he must never suffer his vigilance to relax. When, however, facts come to his knowledge which show that evil has been done, he should not allow disappointment or indignation to influence him. He should realize that he is engaged in working a very radical revolution in facts and in ideas that have held undisputed sway for hundreds of years; that great, even astounding, progress in the desired direction has already been made; but that we are trying in fact to crush into the space of a few years moral and ethical changes which, even among our own energetic countrymen, have been the slow growth of centuries. . . .

Similarly, Political Officers must not be too contemptuous or too intolerant of local superstitions; nor should they regard as "extraordinary" people who hold views very similar to those which were entertained by John Wesley only a hundred and fifty years ago. Some day, no doubt, many of these ideas will be discarded by the natives of Nigeria, as they have now been discarded by ourselves; but the process must inevitably be a very gradual one, and in the mean time the actuality of the native's belief in witchcraft and magic, rather than the soundness or otherwise of his judgement in such matters, should be the fact that should chiefly engross the attention of a Political Officer, since it lends a new meaning and value to acts which are in themselves grossly and inexcusably criminal, if they be judged only from the standpoint of the modern, educated European. . . .

Part Four

❧ EVALUATION

As yet it is too early to judge the effects of imperialism, either upon the imperial powers or upon the colonies. Those who would attempt to strike a clear balance, who can argue passionately that India either would, or definitely would not, have experienced a cottage craft industrial revolution of its own without European interference, or those who conclude that missionaries brought good rather than harm to the islanders of the Pacific, must impose upon such judgments their own largely Western, nation-oriented standards. If they do not come to their task with a view of priorities based upon notions of "modernization," they will come to it with a doctrinaire, deterministic view; this determinism may be economic, geographical, or Providential in nature. Tidy minds do not like untidy conclusions, and to conclude that we cannot, as yet, truly conclude strikes many as a counsel of despair.

Interim judgments, explanations for certain courses of events, even evaluations of specific phases of the colonial experience may nonetheless be possible without locking the door on further and future reevaluations. Such interim efforts, even if not recognized as such by their initiators, are of the nature of sources, providing insights into how a generation, a specific people, or the followers of an *ism* may not only judge imperialism, but use that judgment as a weapon in the ongoing debate—a debate still all too often at the point of someone's bayonet, ideological as well as palpable. The following selections provide several shadings of opinion for those who would view imperialism as either wholly evil or wholly good (and there can be few in either of these two polarized camps). Imperialism remains alive today, as catchword, as slogan, as a verbal artifact which testifies to the period when the Europeanization of the world was at its height.

A Man on the Spot

How did the men charged with administering colonial territories evaluate their own work? How did they receive, judge, and act upon information? The best way to find out, in addition to examining the record of administrators in action, is through the many memoirs and autobiographies the men on the spot left behind. Among British officials alone, such men as Leonard Woolf (in Ceylon early in the twentieth century), A. C. J. Hastings and C. L. Temple (in Nigeria), Sir Alex Grimble (in the Gilbert and Ellice Islands), Sir Bede Clifford and Sir Alan Burns (in the British West Indies), Sir Kenneth Bradley, in his justly famous *Diary of a District Officer* (on Northern Rhodesia), Sir Hugh Foot (in Palestine and Cyprus), Sir Hugh Clifford and Frank Swettenham (in Malaya), Harold Ingrams (in Aden), Sir Henry Luke (in Hong Kong), and H. L. Griffin (in New Guinea) have told us what it was like to be a D. O., administrator, proconsul, and governor. One of the most revealing of these accounts was written by Joyce Cary, who later won fame in the world of letters for his novels, especially *Mister Johnson*. The following extract is drawn from his essay, "Africa Yesterday: One Ruler's Burden."

From *The Case for African Freedom* by Joyce Cary (New York: McGraw-Hill, Inc., 1964), pp. 203–9. The essay used here first appeared in the *Reporter* for May 15, 1951. Reprinted by permission of The University of Texas Press and Curtis Brown Ltd.

It is a great pity that some of our political theorists can't enjoy a short spell as dictators. Nothing is more instructive in the problems of actual government. I have always thought myself lucky to have had such a spell when I was sent, in 1917, to take over Borgu, a remote district of the British colony of Nigeria which at that time had not even a telegraph office. Letters took anything from a week to ten days, according to the state of the Niger and the morale of its ferrymen, for an answer.

I was told, therefore, by my Provincial Resident, Hamilton Brown[e], that I should have to act on my own in any crisis, and rely on him to back me up.

This was not an idle or conventional promise. Some months earlier there had been a rebellion in Borgu. The people had risen, murdered sixty members of their own native administration, and then rushed off to find some British magistrate and state their case.

A friend of mine, Diggle, was sent down to look into it. He found plenty of reason for grievance: extortion, stealing of women, blackmail, corrupt judgments. He turned out the worst offenders and

handed over a peaceful country to me. But he warned me to keep
my eyes open. "You can't get rid of corruption in these parts; you
can only hope to stop it from going on the bust."

Then he went off on leave and left me with my first independent
civil command, in a country of about twelve thousand square miles.
My staff consisted of one clerk who could not spell (we had no type-
writer); twelve police with single-shot carbines and ten rounds apiece;
a Political Agent—a Hausa Negro who spoke the local languages and
was supposed to be an expert on local affairs; and a couple of office
messengers to sun themselves on the court veranda.

Government has been called a relationship. This is a misleading
half-truth. The essence of government, the nub, is rule. That is the
hard part. But it is true that to rule efficiently, a relationship has to
be formed: one of confidence, or fear, or hope, often all three. And
in forming such a relationship the first need is knowledge. My relationship with Hamilton Brown was one of mutual confidence based
on knowledge of each other. Any other would have made my job in
Borgu impossible. But in the other direction I had neither knowledge
nor confidence.

William the Conqueror understood very well what he needed, when
he ordered the Domesday Book compiled. It gave him the foundations
for his system. But I am pretty sure that it gave him no more. He
had to rely for the really important question (not what things people
have in their possession, but what those people are doing with them)
on what he was told from day to day, on opinion, on reports from
spies, on his own guesswork and knowledge of human nature. I am
sure, too, that the success of his rule was not due so much to his
system as to some method by which he did get reliable information
about the working of the system, and the men who worked it. Systems,
ultimately, are men.

My first immediate discovery, quite unexpected in its force, was
that I could not trust anybody or anything—that is, any appearance.
All information was vague, contradictory, palpably false (like the
news of a shipload of Negro nationalists just arrived from the United
States to drive us British into the sea[1]), or trivial. The Wazir (Vizier)
to the Emir came up every day on his official duty to give me the
news and consult upon it, but the Political Agent had different news;
each implied, deviously but resolutely, that the other was a liar. Each
gave broad hints of the other's plots to benefit himself at the expense
of a "new judge"—that is, myself.

My secret-service men, a few ragamuffins recruited by the Political
Agent, either gave wild reports like that of the Negro invasion from
America or told me solemnly that some chief had cursed me, which
I could guess for myself and which did not matter. (As a dictator I

[1] [Back-to-Africa movements were near their height at this time.]

could not pick my own men. Every action of a dictator is watched and known immediately, and if I had chosen an informer he would have been corrupted or beaten up within the same day.)

No one not placed in such a position can fully realize the sense of blindness and distrust which took possession of me in those first months of solitude in Borgu. I say "took possession" because it was at once like a foreign invader seizing on my mind, and a sort of demon. I would wake up at night and feel as if the dark itself were an immense black brain, meditating, behind its thick featureless countenance, some deep plan for a new and still more surprising outbreak.

I could not forget that the last rising had been caused by nothing but the failure of the district officer, in exactly my own position, to know what was going on under his very nose—and that officer had had much more experience than I, and besides had done nothing but his duty. It was the rule then in the Nigerian service, and has always been one of the guiding principles of British colonial policy, to preserve local law and custom as far as possible, and to do nothing that might break the continuity of the local government. Tribal chiefs and tribal councils were to be maintained, and progress made by educating chiefs, by improving their administrative machine, and by a general development of trade, roads, and public services, which (as experience shows) by itself modifies the whole situation and can (if that end is kept in view) quite quickly build up a class capable of some share in the government, on the first elementary representative committees.

But the first principle was absolute: Do not break the continuity. Do not attempt to force a constitution on the people. However good it may seem, however suitable to the place and time (and this is granting a lot), it will be hated and sabotaged. So it will serve only as a bar to all constitutional development.

My predecessor (let's call him Smythe[2]) had done no wrong in supporting the Emir who provoked the rising. He was, I learned, not only astonished but aggrieved when, having been sent on leave in a hurry with acute fever, he heard in England that his people, of whom he was so fond, had burst into revolution as soon as they were left to themselves. He felt that he had been badly treated by fate. I dare say every dictator feels the same in the same case. And in fact Smythe's only fault had been trustfulness and ignorance. He had simply failed to know in time how badly the native administration had been behaving and had failed to use his powers to keep the Emir in order. A political officer, though he must keep in the background, has great power over a chief. He can always warn him, either through his Wazir or at a private interview, that if he does not behave himself

[2] [In fact, it appears that he *was* a Smythe, J. H. G.]

he will be reported to the governor or fined, or even deposed in favor of some other member of the dynasty. On the other hand, a good chief can be rewarded with a raise in pay or some special honor.

Smythe thought that he had a good Emir, a really progressive man. And so, I believe, he had. The Emir was a clever fellow who supported all Smythe's favorite schemes. He perceived that they were actually to his advantage. They cost money, and the more money there was floating about, the more he could steal. In fact, it is just the clever, the active, the really valuable chief who can be most dangerous. How was I to discover that the new Emir, a very distinguished and reserved old gentleman, who had been a slave raider in his time (he had been passed over for the succession partly because of his conservative background and was now brought in as a popular choice to restore public confidence), was not another more sedate and conservative crook?

I remembered the casual remark of an old official that in Africa, even an honest and loyal subordinate never told all the truth to a district officer, because he never knew what use would be made of it.

I realized that the man in absolute power is not only dangerous to all his subjects; he is also a mystery to them. And this, I think now, is true of all men in power. Even the foreman of a labor gang or a senior office clerk is, I suspect, so far as he has power, an uncertain quality to those below. That is to say, the uncertain element in all human relations becomes, in power relations, a source of mistrust. All subordinates say to themselves, "I'll tell the boss no more than I need to—for no one knows what he'll do with it." Everyone in authority has seen in the face of the most trusted subordinate that peculiar look of discretion which means "How much must I give away—how little will satisfy him?" And the greater the power, the more the discretion that surrounds it, even in the stooge, who seems to be within the iron curtain but in fact chooses his words so cunningly.

The way I escaped, simply by good luck, from this invisible jail that shuts off every dictator from the sense and sound of the actual world was still more illuminating. An old friend, my first commanding officer, meeting me by chance on trek and hearing of my difficulty, said that for his part he had found only one method of getting some independent news. He slept always as far as possible from his guard and staff, in a shelter or, during the dry season, alone in the bush. "Your people will never come out into the bush at night, unless they have to—they are much too afraid of ghosts, lions, hyenas, and so on. And as for you, no lion, however hungry, will ever attack a mosquito net. Lions simply don't understand such things."

I took this advice, put my bed under a tree about thirty yards from camp, and after some disappointing weeks suddenly began to have

results. I was waked up about three one morning by a voice whisper-
ing out of the dark, an urgent voice full of bitterness. I don't remember what it said, whether a trivial complaint (one man talked half
the night about a deer into which, he claimed, he had shot the first
arrow and of which he had been cheated of the share due to the
first arrow) or one of the really important ones, such as the revelation
(by an aggrieved petty trader) that a certain chief had closed up fifty
miles of the international frontier with Dahomey. Or more important
still that my Political Agent was in league with this same chief, to
get him special privileges.

But I did in fact, perhaps on a dozen occasions in any one year,
get news. Much of it, of course, was false; all of it needed careful
checking. But what was valuable was of a sort that I could not have
gotten by any other method; and all of it was sufficiently important
to some native to make him take the risk of hostile ghosts, as well as
the ordinary terrors surrounding a dictator.

You may think that this plan, really that of the anonymous letter,
should be beneath the dignity of government. I can only say that a
man with real responsibility for other people's lives and happiness
has no scruples about dignity. And I knew no other way to get the
same results. I saw too that the Lion's Mouth of Venice, via which the
Doges received anonymous denunciations, was not (as the books say)
the wicked device of despots to keep their people in terror; it was an
essential organ of their government, to preserve their own peace of
mind. Of course it was an instrument of terror also. But that is an
unavoidable factor in the whole form of government, in dictatorship
itself. Dictators are always alarming.

This, then, was the first discovery of my dictatorship, that even the
most elementary truths were difficult to come by. The second was
that they suffer a special kind of distortion. Subordinates to any absolute power have a special irresponsibility. Over and over again intelligent men—sub-chiefs, headmen in charge of road or bridge construction—broke out in the stupidest fashion. They suddenly went
on the spree, or having done half a job in a careful and responsible
manner, abandoned or botched the rest. One of them, with a long
and good record, a steady family man, suddenly robbed the pay account in so careless a way that he was at once detected and brought
up for trial. I asked him what had persuaded him to such a folly,
and his only explanation was that gesture, a slight horizontal movement of the hand to and fro, which means, to the Moslem, "As Allah
wills," otherwise "Anything can happen."

What I think is that the fear and uncertainty that pervade every
such régime, as with an atmosphere, breed fatalism. A soldier recognizes the same thing in himself during war service. You have the
paradox that men in daily fear of their lives are therefor more reck-

less than those in safety, and that subordinates under a police state, who can be jailed or shot for a very small fault, are therefor more open to sudden corruption. The enormous corruption of the Nazis and Fascists should not amaze us, and it is easy to understand why the Communists need such frequent purges.

But a still more subtle cause of the treachery infecting every relation in absolute government is the irresistible desire, even among its loyal supporters, to keep things sweet. No one ever gives his immediate boss bad news in its bare form. I can't say how many times I was taken in by reports that seemed, even to my suspicious dictator's mind, clear and exhaustive, but proved to have left out the vital point. The most exasperating and comical was the detailed news of "damage" to a bridge that, when I arrived two days later, was found to have disappeared totally. It was too late to take another road. I had to swim the river, in flood among rocks, and the old chief whom I had brought with me had to be left behind, at the risk of wasting a long, careful negotiation, in which he was to have been the peacemaker, with certain troublesome villages about district boundaries.

I cannot be surprised that Adolf Hitler, toward the end, was fighting battles with armies that had long since ceased to exist.

This disease of absolute government extends in a lesser degree throughout all governmental hierarchies. There is a fatalism in the old bureaucrat that comes not so much from fear as the thought: "This damned setup is so unpredictable anyhow that no one knows what it will do next," and so does not trouble too much about details that probably will be misunderstood or be lost in some pigeonhole. And again there is the tendency to keeps things sweet. . . .

. . . I used to report twice a year on the economic position in Borgu, suggesting possible developments. I would write something like this: "The export of shea butter would be greatly increased by simple improvements at the river port of Leaba, such as a market building. The chief expense would be on the Leaba Road, which for over forty miles has neither any water nor any settlement. At least two villages with wells would be needed, and there are no local welldiggers. I could find hunters ready to settle if wells were provided and three years' tax exemption were offered. Estimate for such a road, complete, with wells and huts for ten families, can be put at x pounds."

In the provincial report for the half year, this would read: "The district officer at Borgu reports that a new river port and market at Leaba would greatly increase the export of shea butter. A new road would be required from Leaba to the capital." That is to say, the qualifications would have been left out to save space and give an encouraging effect. If the suggestion ever reached the Secretary of State for the Colonies, it would be in this form: "A general development of ports on the Niger promises excellent and immediate returns.

This could be achieved with local labor." "Local labor" to the Secretary of State in London would mean merely African labor.

The report writer has to condense. But in the act, he tends, unless he is careful, to leave out more of the drawbacks than the advantages. Otherwise, he runs the risk that some energetic politician on the lookout for positive opportunities will think him a knockover, a Blimp, a stick-in-the-mud, even a secret enemy.

Now I realize why dictators, and even democratic heads of government—Wilson, [Neville] Chamberlain, Roosevelt, Churchill—tend to have confidential advisers, favorites, to send on private missions of inquiry, and to lean heavily on them for information and advice. This, of course, only shifts some power to the favorite, and surrounds him also with walls and distrust. Power does not so much corrupt the ruler as the whole world in which he is compelled to work. It becomes for him, the moment he reaches power, a kind of Castle of Otranto, full of uncertain noises and vague threats, in which the very servants edge away from him as if he had the evil eye. And his friends become favorites, and therefore his closest friends can become his most dangerous enemies. For they, above all, have power, the power to deceive.

A Colonial Officer Looks Back

Civil servants of one nation could not help but compare themselves, and their successes as they saw them, with their counterpart from other nations. One man who attempted to provide a general view of what the governance of white men over non-white had meant on a comparative basis was Walter Russell Crocker, who served extensively in the empire, and most effectively in Nigeria. He then became the Australian High Commissioner (the equivalent of Ambassador) to Kenya. The following is drawn from his post-war appraisal, *On Governing Colonies*.

From *On Governing Colonies: Being an Outline of the Real Issues and a Comparison of the British, French and Belgian Approach to Them* by Walter Russell Crocker (London: George Allen & Unwin Ltd., 1947), pp. 138–48. Reprinted by permission of the publisher.

All the Colonial Powers in Africa have done well by their African wards. The sense of responsibility is particularly active among the French, the Belgians, and the British; in the last twenty years it has grown from strength to strength. Imperialism in the ugly sense is, over the greatest part of Africa, dead. . . . There are enough authentic problems in Africa without getting emotional over what does not exist.

The Belgian approach to their colonial responsibilities is too similar to the British to call for further comment here. The problems in the Congo are less complicated than in most of Africa, and the Belgians are free to concentrate on them without having to disperse their energies over the wide and diverse fields which the French and British are required to cover. The ratio between population and economic resources in the Congo is also in their favour. Sometimes it looks as though their aims go no further than turning their Africans into healthy cattle, but that is a superficial view. Despite a feet-on-the-earth realism, both their policy and their practice are much concerned with the quality of life, now and in the future. Their difficulties will arise when the Bantu awakens to political consciousness. For the time being it is sufficient to say that what they are doing is as good as anything being done in Africa. . . .

As between the British and the French approach to their respective colonial responsibilities there is, on the other hand, a fundamental difference.

The approach of either is determined by the national temperament.

The dominant political strain in the British national temperament and tradition is whiggery; in the French it is Jacobinism. Whiggery heavily impregnates British colonial policy and practice; Jacobinism heavily impregnates French. And so too with other manifestations of the national temperament: in the British colonies, for example, besides the parliamentary idea and Gladstonian administrative rules and *ad hoc* liberalism, our cricket matches and blazers and clubs and dinner jackets and Churches are, like our language, there for good, whatever may be the fate of our suzerainty.

Everything considered the British effort, I believe, is better now and more promising for the future than the French. It is not pleasant for anyone who feels a respect and an affection for France to criticize the French colonial effort, all the more so when the French are so proud of and so sensitive about it, and when, too, it has so much, like its medical work and its generous disregard of colour prejudice, to its credit. Nevertheless I see no escape from passing a judgment that is less favourable to the French than it is to the British.

British policy starts from the point that the African is the end himself. There is no *arrière pensee* about it. Whatever its shortcomings may be in conscious theorizing, it does seek to achieve for him the maximum welfare possible now and to give him self-government as soon as he can exercise it. We may be muddled but we see ourselves as Trustees who are to hand over their trust at the earliest practicable moment. French policy, on the other hand, is not muddled but it starts from the point that what matters most is not the African but France. It never rids itself of preoccupations about military manpower, war supplies, strategic bases. The end is not the African but what he can contribute to France's political-military position as a World Power. We too, of course, also think of our political-military position. The strategic value of our colony of Gambia, for example, is not likely to be overlooked; and still less that of Freetown. But the African nevertheless remains for us the first priority. . . .

To the friendly foreign observer it seems likely that France, thanks to this uncompromising and unrealistic hostility to any sort of political devolution in her Empire, and oddly enough also thanks to the spirit of social Jacobinism, will have more political troubles than will the British, and she will reap more hatred in the process. The likelihood is the greater because it is far from certain whether the virtues of the French (derived, notwithstanding the adultness of French civilization and the mature brilliance of individuals, essentially from a peasant and small-country outlook) are the kind required for the detailed organization of a vast and vastly diversified Empire into so highly centralized a bloc. There is nothing in the French Government system anywhere to show it. Further, the only way the policy of the *Union Française* could work with certainty would be to give more or less complete equality to all within it. The French would then be a minority in their *Union Française*.[1]

Whether there will be or will not be political upheavals in the future, it is certain that the policy of impatient frenchification and its resulting assault on native society, inspired by this permanent pre-occupation with the political-military position of France, has made life less agreeable for the African in French colonies than in British. The policy has not got as far in practice as the French desire or claim, partly because of the poverty of their colonies (which has slowed down all plans), partly because of the passive resistance of the African, and partly because of the good sense of their officials out in the bush on whom the day-to-day business of government falls.

In practice there is thus some blurring of the differences between the lot of the average bush African on one side of the Anglo-French frontier and the other; in the bush the similarities of practice are often greater than the differences. The *Administrateur* at Tessawa, for example, goes about his work very much the same way as his British colleague across the border at Daura. But the difference in conception remains, and even there in the interior, far from capitals and ports and the Europeanized Africans, the difference finds expression in a multitude of small ways which are not lost on the native.

The British share one great defect with the French: the way they conceive of "Development."

British efforts for progress in Africa have been marred by two major shortcomings. First, we see things from the wrong end. Our perspective is false. Thus we spend £X on a hospital when £X/2 would have given the locality concerned a water supply, the lack of which causes more diseases than the hospital could ever hope to deal with; or we lavish energy on devising a constitution which might mollify the demands of a handful of town lawyers and clerks when we have made no more than a beginning on self-government in the villages; or we orientate our Agricultural Departments into spending themselves on some special unrepresentative activity when nothing is done for the ordinary self-subsistent peasant; or we "reform" a judicial system in order to better the lot of professional lawyers. . . . Second, and it flows on from the first, we lack the unified attack. None of these colonial problems can be isolated from the rest. They are parts of a living whole. That is why the Tennessee Valley Authority with its conception and its practice of the total and the integrated approach contains a lesson of the highest relevance to Colonies. Starting from the base of the self-subsistent peasant you set all your departments going on the essential tasks such as water, seeds, pests, animals, co-operatives, village government, village schools, and from there the budget of roads and railways and industries and higher education and

[1] [As the British—and white Dominions—have become in the Commonwealth.]

central self-government can be dealt with in their natural order; which is to say, as and as far as they are rooted in the primordial purpose—the self-subsistent peasant. Policy should grow from the soil, like a tree.

The starting point is the people, the real people and what they most need. It is for this reason that policy in Africa cannot be shaped by considerations of what is best in the West Indies. Beyond the fact that the West Indies are Crown Colonies and that most West Indians are black in colour there is little if anything in common between the problems of Africa and those of the West Indies.

This habit of comparing peoples and places that are not comparable is largely to blame for our rushing the African faster than is good for him. The overhasty introduction, not to say imposition, of our legal concepts and procedure is a case in point. Other examples are legion. A recent example is the way in which trade unions were introduced by the Government in Nigeria. Concepts and practices were taken over *en bloc* from England and imposed on the irrelevant conditions obtaining in Nigeria. In 1945, three or four years later, the Government had on its hands a General Strike which had been launched with an irresponsibility that would have been comical had it not been dangerous. . . .

In the last analysis the fundamental question in colonial policy today is the question of introducing European civilization among primitive peoples.

It is strange that almost everyone assumes that there is no question about it at all, and that our first duty is to spread the blessings of our way of life as quickly as possible.

No decision on colonial policy, therefore, is worth anything unless it is grounded firmly on a clear understanding of what our civilization is and of what African civilization is.

As for our civilization, can any man of sense and sensibility have lived through the last twenty years and still retain a confident conviction as to the superior value of our way of life or as to the promise of its future? Our technological advances hold out a prospect of mastering poverty and insecurity and drudgery and disease, at all events in their main incidents. All we need to do is to control our technological skills. Perhaps we will control them. But until we have got further ahead in that direction than now, it is wiser to keep in mind the present poverty and insecurity of life for most Europeans, the present incidence of disease, the present huge social inequalities, the frustration in work, the loneliness, the emptiness of life, and the murderous intolerances. We might achieve a golden future. Here and now the best of our townsman's world has been exposed in the Lynds' *Middletown;* the worst has been exposed by the war. It is a tale told by an idiot. And he is a bold optimist who can exclude from his vision of the future flame-throwers, stratosphere rockets, arsene gases, ten-ton bombs, inextinguishable incendiaries, atomic explosives, and all the other utensils in the Devil's Kitchen within our grasp. A wry smile must surely rise on the faces of the gods as they watch the irony of the position, for the unhappiest age in recorded history is spurred with a missionary urge to spread its way of life on a people whom it commiserates as unfortunate.

As for the African way of life, the African suffers from poverty, it is true, like most of mankind; but the absolute poverty is less than in much of Europe and in most of Asia and the relative poverty (relative to his needs, material and psychological) is less than the poverty of Europeans. Like most of mankind he also suffers from disease, but his health both physically and psychologically is above that of the average European. And he derives more interest from his daily work, his basic beliefs are more rooted, his family life is more stable and his society is closer-knit, warmer, and less unequal, than that of the European. He has not attained unto painless dentistry, scientific surgery, wireless sets, automobiles, and the rest, but make no mistake about it, the average African gets more joy from his life than the average European. . . .

It is true enough that we cannot conceal our civilization from him. Much of it, moreover, we cannot deny to him: we have in any case gone too far for that. Thus mass literacy is on its way. But there are two facts to remember in this connection. One is that the vast majority of Africans, perhaps as many as three in every four, still live in small villages, tilling their own farms or herding their flocks or working at their ancient crafts, and thinking their own thoughts and following the old rules of life. The new *élite* in Lagos, Dakar or Elisabethville is more noisy than numerous. The other fact is that we, the Trustee Powers, can control and direct both the volume and the speed of the inflow of our civilization. We are not as helpless as all that.

The African himself must understand that if he insists on a high standard of living, which is to say on purchasing power, he must pay the price. The price is his own independence. He will get this purchasing power if in industrial production he goes into factories or mines and becomes a wage earner, or if in agriculture he goes in for capitalized plantations on the one hand, or socialized collective farming on the other, and becomes a controlled unit in these aggregations.

For the green felt hats, coloured sweaters, gramophones, wireless sets, motor-cycles, cameras, and so up to frigidaires, motor-cars, cinemas, here is the price he must pay—freedom. The bulk of the literates are clamouring for these things; perhaps most of the unsophisticated would blindly surrender their freedom for them. The great voluntary stream of labourers from Central Africa, where they have freedom but no green hats, down into the Union [of South Africa], where they have no freedom but can get green hats, is illustrative. The Congo, too, shows with what readiness the African will surrender his independence in return for the higher material standard of living he can get as a mine worker, a factory worker, or a planation worker. But we, the Trustees, can and must help the African before this dilemma. . . .

Let us then give him those of our techniques in which he stands in genuine need, but let us clear our minds of cant as to what our civilization is worth and as to what his is worth. The African has produced no Belsen camps.[2] . . .

Peoples of countries which are responsible for running colonies must clear their minds of misinformation and cant. Perhaps in time it will not be too much to hope that peoples of other countries will clear their minds of at least some of the grosser misinformation and some of the grosser cant now current about colonial affairs. A beginning might well be made by banning the portmanteau bogey word *imperialism*. If this is asking too much then let the word cease to be linked with Britain alone. The spreading of strategic or political or economic hegemony by our Russian friends in Eastern Europe seems to be very much like what they denounce as imperialism in Gambia or Senegal; and the demands of our American friends to the Marshalls, Carolines, and other strategic *points d'appui* in the Pacific, to say nothing of the whole Carribean Region or of Liberia, and to say still less of dollar diplomacy, seems to be very much like what they denounce as imperialism in Ceylon or Java. Moreover, this imperialism of either our Russian or our American friends shows little evidence of "the paramountcy of native interests" which is the mainspring of British Colonial Policy. Korea is now divided up between the Russians and the Americans: there is no evidence that in either the Russian zone or the American zone the interests of Koreans are treated as paramount. Is it possible that the difference between British or Belgian imperialism on the one hand and Russian or American imperialism on the other consists in the attitude of responsibility of the former for their colonial charges and of irresponsibility of the latter for theirs?

[2] [This was, of course, written long before the war for Biafran independence.]

The View of an Asian Scholar
and Diplomat

Sardar Kavalam Madhava Panikkar has been one of India's most prolific historians. Educated in the East at Madras University, and in the West, at Oxford, Panikkar was also a lawyer, the editor of the highly influential *Hindustan Times,* and India's ambassador to China, Egypt, and France. A nationalist, and a poet in his native Malayalam, Panikkar wrote one of the major interpretive accounts of the imperial experience, *Asia and Western Dominance,* after World War II. He died in 1963.

From *Asia and Western Dominance: A Survey of the Vasco Da Gama Epoch of Asian History, 1498–1945* by K. M. Panikkar (London: George Allen & Unwin Ltd., 1959), pp. 314–20. Reprinted by permission of the publisher.

. . . The upsurge in the Catholic religion, of which the most characteristic expression was the Society of Jesus, saw in the East great prospects of evangelization. The Portuguese monarchy was deeply influenced by this, and we have from this time a new urge which sent Jesuit fathers to the courts of the Grand Mogul, the Chinese Emperor and the Shogun. This urge weakened a little with the arrival of the Dutch and the English in Asian waters, for till the beginning of the nineteenth century Protestant churches did not feel the call of converting the heathen and entering seriously into the mission field. But in the nineteenth century, and up to the First European War, evangelization again becomes a major urge in European relations with Asia. It may indeed be said that the most serious, persistent and planned effort of European nations in the nineteenth century was their missionary activities in India and China, where a large-scale attempt was made to effect a mental and spiritual conquest as supplementing the political authority already enjoyed by Europe. Though the results were disappointing in the extreme from the missionary point of view, this assault on the spiritual foundations of Asian countries has had far-reaching consequences in the religious and social reorganization of the peoples. . . . Indeed, it might be appropriately said that while political aggrandisement was the work of governments and groups, and commerce the interest of organized capital, mission work was the effort of the people of the West to bring home to the masses of Asia their view of the values of life.

Religion, however, was only one aspect of European expansion.

148

Even with the Portuguese, who in the beginning equated the establishment of a monopoly in spice trade with religion, trade soon over-
shadowed the religious aspect of their work. With the arrival of the
Protestant Powers trade became for a time the only consideration.
There was little contact outside commercial relations. If by an Act of
God the relations of Europe with Asia had ceased all of a sudden in
1748, little would have been left to show for two and a-half centuries
of furious activity. Even in India, there would have only been a few
ruined forts on unfrequented coasts, some churches erected also in
coastal areas by the Portuguese, a small community of half-castes,
regretting the days when they were people of prestige—hardly anything more. In the trading period, 1610–1758, Europe influenced Asia
but little.

In the period of conquest (1750–1857), however, the situation began
to change. Asian leaders began to feel that the strangers had become
a menace and had to be taken seriously. It is not surprising that the
first serious interest that the Asian leaders began to show was in
cannon-making, army organization and military equipment. But apart
from this justifiable curiosity in respect of military matters shown by
a few people in power, there were others who were interested in the
intellectual and spiritual strength of the European nations. Ram
Mohan Roy and his school in India and the Rangakusha school in
Japan are examples of this changing attitude towards Europe. Citizen
Tipoo as a member of the Jacobin Club of Seringapatam, Ram Mohan
Roy in correspondence with the leaders of the Enlightenment in
Europe, and public meetings in Calcutta to congratulate the liberal
revolutionaries in Spain were symptoms of an intellectual awakening
and a sense of world-community which was dawning on Asia.

The most significant single factor which changed the intellectual
relationship of Europe and Asia was the French Revolution. Few
people today realize the immense influence of the French Revolution
outside Europe. Negroes in Haiti, Tipoo in Mysore, Dutch radicals
in Indonesia, all felt the ripples of this movement. The reforms of
[Marshal Herman Willen] Dandaels in Java were a direct result of
it. [The Marquis of] Wellesley's aggressive policy leading to the conquest and annexation of large areas of India was one of its indirect
consequences, for it was the fear of the revolutionary French that
provided the main motive of his policy of conquest. But it is not in
this sense that the doctrines of the French Revolution—"liberty,
equality and fraternity"—came to have a pervading influence on Asia.
As a revolution the developments in France had but little immediate
influence on the Asian people. In the period that followed the Napoleonic experiment, the doctrines of the Revolution had become the
common inheritance of European liberalism. Modified and made re-
spectable by the reformers in the period immediately following the

Napoleonic era, they became the mental background of European statesmen. Education could no longer be neglected in the possessions of European nations. Codes of modern law had to be provided; and even the Dutch had to pay lip service to the interests of the Indonesians when they recovered the lost colony of Java. Slowly a liberal tradition penetrated the policies of European nations.

Not only did the French revolutionary doctrines become in due course an influence on European thought in relation to the East, but they provided the Asian peoples with their first political ideology. Indian writings of the first period of nationalism hark back to the principles of this school. Ram Mohan Roy and his followers, petitioning for the abolition of *Suttee,* for education in English, for greater freedom for women, though they quote from Hindu scriptures in justification of their reforms, are really thinking in terms of [Jean-Jacques] Rousseau, watered down to meet Indian conditions. European inspiration of the Asian reform movements of the first half of the nineteenth century cannot be denied.

The nineteenth century witnessed the apogee of capitalism in Europe. That this was in a large measure due to Europe's exploitation of Asian resources is now accepted by historians. As Hobson, the historian of Imperialism, observes: "The exploitation of other portions of the world, through military plunder, unequal trade and forced labour, has been the one great indispensable condition in the growth of European capitalism." It is the riches of Asian trade (and American) flowing to Europe that enabled the great industrial revolution to take place in England. But with the establishment of capitalism as the dominant economic structure of the colonizing nations, an immense and far-reaching change took place in the relations of the West with Asia. In the eighteenth century, conquest was for the purpose of trade. In the area you conquered, you excluded other nations, bought at the cheapest price, organized production by forced labour to suit your requirements, and transferred the profits to the mother country. In the nineteenth century conquest was not for trade but for investment. Tea plantations and railway construction became major interests in Britain's connection with India. Vast sums were invested in India for building railways. "Of the loans for Indian Railways," says an English writer, "about one-third went to pay the home charges in London, something under one-third was spent on wages and administrative expenses, largely paid to English engineers, and something over one-third on British rails and engines and in paying British ships to bring them to India."

The third phase of European relations with Asia, which begins with the middle of the nineteenth century, is the period of imperialism in the true sense of the word. The transformation is completed earliest in India, which provides the pattern for the rest, for the

Dutch in Indonesia, for the French in Indo-China, for all the nations in respect of China. The imperialist relationship, involving large-scale capital investment, had the result of importing into Asia advanced technical skills and scientific knowledge. Railway construction, which was the main field of capital investment, required the importation of engineers. Rivers had to be spanned, tunnels had to be built, and the lines, once constructed, had to be maintained. Imported technical skill, except at the highest levels, became too costly, and as a result engineering colleges and schools became unavoidable. The spread of technical knowledge in the East, of which this is merely an example, was a necessary result of capital investment. It was not possible to keep Asian nationals out of this knowledge, for returns on capital depended on finding technical skill locally. In regard to industry also, a similar movement became noticeable. European industries established in Calcutta, Bombay and Shanghai had to depend, at least in their lower levels, on locally trained personnel. With the advancement of knowledge among local populations it became impossible to prevent Asian capital from encroaching on European industrial monopolies. In India, cotton mills began to spring up in Bombay and Ahmedabad. In Shanghai, which had become practically a European city, Chinese industrialists found no difficulty in setting up factories in imitation of European models. Railway construction in China, which was a subject of furious international competition, when it was first taken up, soon became an activity of the Chinese Government. Thus, in its primary aspect, imperialism as an export of capital carried into Asia the seeds of its own destruction.

In its second aspect, that is territorial expansion for providing areas for exploitation, European imperialism in the nineteenth century, under the humanitarian impulses of the liberal movement, embarked on a policy of education, welfare schemes and even political training. Direct administration of vast populations naturally created new interests. The administrative authorities had no direct connection with or interest in trade, the officers being, at least according to English tradition, recruited from the middle classes with public school training. So in India, and to some extent in Indonesia, a contradiction developed within the structure of imperialism in which the administrative authorities were inclined to emphasize the welfare aspect of their work, while the commercial interests still considered the territories as areas for exploitation. . . . Nor was it less apparent in places where the power [was] exercised indirectly as in China. The bitter controversies between the Shanghai and treaty port merchants' opinion on the one hand and the Foreign Office on the other in dealing with China . . . is another instance of this contradiction. In fact political authority, combined with the humanitarian ideals of the era of peace, brought a sense of responsibility towards "the backward peoples." No danger to the supremacy of Europe was suspected as being inherent in this development, for even at the end of the nineteenth century the Europeans—even the most progressive among them —were convinced that their superiority was divinely ordained and was safe at least for centuries to come. The idea that the Chinese, weak, immobilized and without industrial potential, could stand up and fight the European within a measurable time, or that Indians could compete with the British in trade or industry, or that the hundreds of Indonesian islands could be united in opposition to the Dutch, would have sounded ludicrous to a European in the Augustan age of imperialism. Therefore the humanitarian ideal of educating the Asian people and of encouraging them to develop at least those skills which were necessary for the more effective discharge of the white man's mission, was pursued without any sense of fear.

Also, the complexities of direct administration of vast areas like India and Indonesia made it necessary to develop a large body of indigenous administrative personnel. In the period of trade there was no such necessity. In the period of imperialism this was unavoidable.

The apparatus of modern States, run largely by local talent, had to be built up, providing the Asian peoples both with administrative training and with knowledge and understanding of the mechanism of modern government. This is particularly important, for one of the main differences between the earlier periods of history and the political systems that developed in the nineteenth and twentieth centuries lay in the vast administrative systems which touched every aspect of life which the State organizations of the nineteenth and twentieth centuries represented. In the eighteenth century, neither in Europe nor in Asia was there a government which was also an administration in the present-day sense. In the latter half of the nineteenth century European countries, having had to deal with more and more complex problems of industry, commerce, social and economic welfare, organized the vast mechanism of modern administration, which neither Frederick the Great nor Napoleon could have conceived, and which earlier political thought would have resisted bitterly as encroachments on liberty.

The Asian State-systems though essentially bureaucratic and therefore "administrative" and not political, were, however, limited to land administration and defence. The administrative system which the Crown developed in India and which every colonial administration felt compelled to develop in its territory, not only provided the first conception of the modern State to the Asian mind, but equipped it with the mechanism necessary to realize it in time. . . .

The third aspect of territorial expansion—of the era of imperialism —was the popular sentiment of responsibility for "moral wellbeing" which found its most characteristic expression in the missionary work.

The conscience of the people, especially of the Protestant countries, was aroused by the fact that in the areas directly governed by them or under their influence hundreds of millions lived and died without the chance of salvation. . . . Though the results of their religious activities were negligible and often led only to reactions which they least expected, their interest in the life and wellbeing of the common people, and their efforts to break down the barrier of race, had the benefit of bringing the West nearer to Asia. Also, their educational and medical work in the interior of India, China and Burma had far-reaching consequences.

It is necessary to emphasize that the contact between the peoples of the East with Europeans began really only in the era of imperialism. In the 300 and odd years that preceded it (from 1498 to 1858) this contact was limited, even in India, to narrow circles, and had not penetrated even into the ruling classes. With direct administration, development of educational systems, exploitation instead of trade, the contact gradually extended to different levels. Slowly Asian youths began to find their way to European seats of learning. . . . The first impulse which took young Indians across the seas was not to probe the mysteries of European life, but the more material consideration of a chance to compete in the Civil Service examinations. But soon this movement assumed immense proportions, and a large proportion of the students who went to Europe were dedicated to the study of such subjects as engineering, medicine, forestry, geology and chemistry apart, of course, from law and social sciences. A similar movement took large numbers of Indo-Chinese students to Paris and Indonesians to Leyden. The prestige of German technical advances attracted a growing number to the universities of the Reich.

The essential point for our purpose is that in every one of the countries of Asia, the leadership in the movement which ultimately displaced European supremacy belonged to those who had been trained by the West under the aegis of imperialism. Not only Mahatma Gandhi and Jawaharlal Nehru, but the founders of the Indian National Congress and the successive generations of Congress leaders were trained in the West. In Japan, it was the group of explorers sent to the West by the Shogunate that led the movement for the reorganization of the State. In China, though the deposition of the Manchus was not the work of Western-educated people, the building up of the revolutionary movement that followed was led by men of Western training. In Indonesia, Indo-China, Burma and Ceylon it is the men and women educated in the West . . . that provided the leadership.

It will thus be seen that in the relationship between the East and the West, the vital period which witnessed the realization of European ambitions and generated at the same time the movements which led to its destruction was the period of Imperialism. . . .

The Voice of the Damned

But who would speak for the masses, for the inarticulate, exploited, native peasantry? Was this even an appropriate way to refer to indigenous populations, who were also to be thought of as the benefited, rising proletariat *cum* middle class? The most articulate, and passionate, voice to speak for those who were at the receiving end of colonialism, who were brutalized by the presence of decision-makers who ignored local needs or wishes, was that of a brilliant Negro psychiatrist who, as a French-trained doctor, worked in Algeria. Born in Martinique, interested at first in the idea of *négritude*, and author in 1952 of *Peau noire, masques blancs* (*Black Faces, White Masks*), Frantz Fanon turned his back on his assured status in Algeria as a French citizen and doctor and joined the revolution, becoming the ambassador to Ghana from the Provisional Government of the Algerian Republic. He died of leukemia, in 1961, at the age of thirty-six, and was buried in the country whose independence he helped secure.

Fanon was especially concerned with the problem of violence in modern society. During the last year of his life he wrote *Les Damnés de la terre,* seeing the book into print a month before he died. An immediate success, it led Africanists to place Fanon's name with those of Victor Hugo, Rousseau, and Lenin. Posthumously Fanon's articles were collected for publication, and they are said to have helped Ben Bella to shape his Algerian reforms of 1963 and unquestionably have had a major impact on the civil rights movement in the United States, as well as on insurgency warfare in Africa. The following selections are drawn from two of these books, *The Wretched of the Earth* (*Les Damnés*) and *Studies in a Dying Colonialism.*

From *The Wretched of the Earth* by Frantz Fanon, trans. Constance Farrington (New York: Grove Press, Inc., 1965), pp. 59–76. Copyright © 1963 by *Presence Africaine.* Reprinted by permission of Grove Press, Inc., and MacGibbon & Kee.

Nowadays a theoretical problem of prime importance is being set, on the historical plane as well as on the level of political tactics, by the liberation of the colonies: when can one affirm that the situation is ripe for a movement of national liberation? In what form should it first be manifested? Because the various means whereby decolonization has been carried out have appeared in many different aspects, reason hesitates and refuses to say which is a true decolonization, and which a false. We shall see that for a man who is in the thick of the fight it is an urgent matter to decide on the means and the tactics to employ: that is to say, how to conduct and organize the movement. If this coherence is not present there is only a blind will toward freedom, with the terribly reactionary risks which it entails.

What are the forces which in the colonial period open up new outlets and engender new aims for the violence of colonized peoples? In the first place there are the political parties and the intellectual or commercial elites. Now, the characteristic feature of certain political structures is that they proclaim abstract principles but refrain from issuing definite commands. The entire action of these nationalist political parties during the colonial period is action of the electoral type: a string of philosophico-political dissertations on the themes of the rights of peoples to self-determination, the rights of man to freedom from hunger and human dignity, and the unceasing affirmation of the principle: "One man, one vote." The national political parties never lay stress upon the necessity of a trial of armed strength, for the good reason that their objective is not the radical overthrowing of the system. Pacifists and legalists, they are in fact partisans of order, the new order—but to the colonialist bourgeoisie they put bluntly enough the demand which to them is the main one: "Give us more power." On the specific question of violence, the elite are ambiguous. They are violent in their words and reformist in their attitudes. When the nationalist political leaders *say* something, they make quite clear that they do not really *think* it.

This characteristic on the part of the nationalist political parties should be interpreted in the light both of the make-up of their leaders and the nature of their followings. The rank-and-file of a nationalist party is urban. The workers, primary schoolteachers, artisans, and small shop keepers who have begun to profit—at a discount, to be sure—from the colonial setup, have special interests at heart. What this sort of following demands is the betterment of their particular lot: increased salaries, for example. The dialogue between these political parties and colonialism is never broken off. Improvements are discussed, such as full electoral representation, the liberty of the press, and liberty of association. Reforms are debated. Thus it need not astonish anyone to notice that a large number of natives are militant members of the branches of political parties which stem from the mother country. These natives fight under an abstract watchword: "Government by the workers," and they forget that in their country it should be *nationalist* watchwords which are first in the field. The native intellectual has clothed his aggressiveness in his barely veiled desire to assimilate himself to the colonial world. He has used his aggressiveness to serve his own individual interests.

Thus there is very easily brought into being a kind of class of affranchised slaves, or slaves who are individually free. What the intellectual demands is the right to multiply the emancipated, and the opportunity to organize a genuine class of emancipated citizens. On the other hand, the mass of the people have no intention of standing by and watching individuals increase their chances of success. What they demand is not the settler's position of status, but the settler's place. The immense majority of natives want the settler's farm. For them, there is no question of entering into competition with the settler. They want to take his place.

The peasantry is systematically disregarded for the most part by the propaganda put out by the nationalist parties. And it is clear that in the colonial countries the peasants alone are revolutionary, for they have nothing to lose and everything to gain. The starving peasant, outside the class system, is the first among the exploited to discover that only violence pays. For him there is no compromise, no possible coming to terms; colonization and decolonization are simply a question of relative strength. The exploited man sees that his liberation implies the use of all means, and that of force first and foremost. When in 1956, after the capitulation of Monsieur Guy Mollet to the settlers in Algeria, the Front de Libération Nationale, in a famous leaflet, stated that colonialism only loosens its hold when the knife is at its throat, no Algerian really found these terms too violent. The leaflet only expressed what every Algerian felt at heart: colonialism is not a thinking machine, nor a body endowed with reasoning faculties. It is violence in its natural state, and it will only yield when confronted with greater violence.

At the decisive moment, the colonialist bourgeoisie, which up till then has remained inactive, comes into the field. It introduces that new idea which is in proper parlance a creation of the colonial situation: non-violence. In its simplest form this non-violence signifies to the intellectual and economic elite of the colonized country that the bourgeoisie has the same interests as they and that it is therefore urgent and indispensable to come to terms for the public good. Non-violence is an attempt to settle the colonial problem around a green baize table, before any regrettable act has been performed or irreparable gesture made, before any blood has been shed. But if the masses, without waiting for the chairs to be arranged around the baize table, listen to their own voice and begin committing outrages and setting fire to buildings, the elite and the nationalist bourgeois parties will be seen rushing to the colonists to exclaim, "This is very serious! We do not know how it will end; we must find a solution—some sort of compromise."

This idea of compromise is very important in the phenomenon of decolonization, for it is very far from being a simple one. Compromise involves the colonial system and the young nationalist bourgeoisie at one and the same time. The partisans of the colonial system discover that the masses may destroy everything. Blow-up bridges, ravaged farms, repressions, and fighting harshly disrupt the economy. Compromise is equally attractive to the nationalist bourgeoisie, who since they are not clearly aware of the possible consequences of the rising storm, are genuinely afraid of being swept away by this huge hurricane and never stop saying to the settlers: "We are still capable of stopping the slaughter; the masses still have confidence in us; act quickly if you do not want to put everything in jeopardy." One step more, and the leader of the nationalist party keeps his distance with regard to that violence. He loudly proclaims that he has nothing to do with these Mau-Mau, these terrorists, these throat-slitters. At best, he shuts himself off in a no man's land between the terrorists and the settlers and willingly offers his services as go-between; that is to say, that as the settlers cannot discuss terms with these Mau-Mau, he himself will be quite willing to begin negotiations. Thus it is that the rear guard of the national struggle, that very party of people who have never ceased to be on the other side in the fight, find themselves somersaulted into the van of negotiations and compromise—precisely because that party has taken very good care never to break contact with colonialism.

Before negotiations have been set afoot, the majority of nationalist parties confine themselves for the most part to explaining and excusing this "savagery." They do not assert that the people have to use physical force, and it sometimes even happens that they go so far as to condemn, in private, the spectacular deeds which are declared to be hateful by the press and public opinion in the mother country. The legitimate excuse for this ultra-conservative policy is the desire to see things in an objective light; but this traditional attitude of the native intellectual and of the leaders of the nationalist parties is not, in reality, in the least objective. For in fact they are not at all convinced that this impatient violence of the masses is the most efficient means of defending their own interests. Moreover, there are some individuals who are convinced of the ineffectiveness of violent methods; for them, there is no doubt about it, every attempt to break colonial oppression by force is a hopeless effort, an attempt at suicide, because in the innermost recesses of their brains the settler's tanks and airplanes occupy a huge place. . . . They are beaten from the start. There is no need to demonstrate their incapacity to triumph by violent methods; they take it for granted in their everyday life and in their political maneuvers. They have remained in the same childish position as Engels took up in his famous polemic with that monument of puerility, Monsieur Duhring:

> In the same way that Robinson (Crusoe) was able to obtain a sword, we can just as well suppose that (Man) Friday might appear one fine morning with a loaded revolver in his hand, and from then on the whole relationship of violence is reversed: Man Friday gives the orders and Crusoe is obliged to work. . . . Thus, the revolver triumphs over the sword, and even the most childish believer in axioms will

doubtless form the conclusion that violence is not a simple act of will, but needs for its realization certain very concrete preliminary conditions, and in particular the implements of violence; and the more highly developed of these implements will carry the day against primitive ones. Moreover, the very fact of the ability to produce such weapons signifies that the producer of highly developed weapons, in everyday speech the arms manufacturer, triumphs over the producer of primitive weapons. To put it briefly, the triumph of violence depends upon the production of armaments, and this in its turn depends on production in general, and thus . . . on economic strength, on the economy of the State, and in the last resort on the material means which that violence commands.[1]

In fact, the leaders of reform have nothing else to say than: "With what are you going to fight the settlers? With your knives? Your shotguns?"

It is true that weapons are important when violence comes into play, since all finally depends on the distribution of these implements. But it so happens that the liberation of colonial countries throws new light on the subject. For example, we have seen that during the Spanish campaign, which was a very genuine colonial war, Napoleon, in spite of an army which reached in the offensives of the spring of 1810 the huge figure of 400,000 men, was forced to retreat. Yet the French army made the whole of Europe tremble by its weapons of war, by the bravery of its soldiers, and by the military genius of its leaders. Face to face with the enormous potentials of the Napoleonic troops, the Spaniards, inspired by an unshakeable national ardor, rediscovered the famous methods of guerilla warfare which, twenty-five years before, the American militia had tried out on the English forces. But the native's guerilla warfare would be of no value as opposed to other means of violence if it did not form a new element in the worldwide process of competition between trusts and monopolies.

In the early days of colonization, a single column could occupy immense stretches of country: the Congo, Nigeria, the Ivory Coast, and so on. Today, however, the colonized countries' national struggle crops up in a completely new international situation. Capitalism, in its early days, saw in the colonies a source of raw materials which, once turned into manufactured goods, could be distributed on the European market. After a phase of accumulation of capital, capitalism has today come to modify its conception of the profit-sharing capacity of a commercial enterprise. The colonies have become a market. The colonial population is a customer who is ready to buy goods; consequently, if the garrison has to be perpetually reinforced, if buying and selling slackens off, that is to say if manufactured and finished

---

[1] Friedrich Engels: *Anti-Dühring*, Part II, Chapter III, "Theory of Violence," p. 199 [original note].

goods can no longer be exported, there is clear proof that the solution of military force must be set aside. A blind domination founded on slavery is not economically speaking worthwhile for the bourgeoisie of the mother country. The monopolistic group within this bourgeoisie does not support a government whose policy is solely that of the sword. What the factory-owners and finance magnates of the mother country expect from their government is not that it should decimate the colonial peoples, but that it should safeguard with the help of economic conventions their own "legitimate interests."

Thus there exists a sort of detached complicity between capitalism and the violent forces which blaze up in colonial territory. What is more, the native is not alone against the oppressor, for indeed there is also the political and diplomatic support of progressive countries and peoples. But above all there is competition, that pitiless war which financial groups wage upon each other. A Berlin Conference was able to tear Africa into shreds and divide her up between three or four imperial flags. At the moment, the important thing is not whether such-and-such a region in Africa is under French or Belgian sovereignty, but rather that the economic zones are respected. Today, wars of repression are no longer waged against rebel sultans; everything is more elegant, less bloodthirsty; the liquidation of the Castro regime will be quite peaceful. They do all they can to strangle Guinea and they eliminate Mossadegh. Thus the nationalist leader who is frightened of violence is wrong if he imagines that colonialism is going to "massacre all of us." The military will of course go on playing with tin soldiers which date from the time of the conquest, but higher finance will soon bring the truth home to them.

This is why reasonable nationalist political parties are asked to set out their claims as clearly as possible, and to seek with their colonialist opposite numbers, calmly and without passion, for a solution which will take the interests of both parties into consideration. We see that if this nationalist reformist tendency which often takes the form of a kind of caricature of trade unionism decides to take action, it will only do so in a highly peaceful fashion, through stoppages of work in the few industries which have been set up in the towns, mass demonstrations to cheer the leaders, and the boycotting of buses or of imported commodities. All these forms of action serve at one and the same time to bring pressure to bear on the forces of colonialism, and to allow the people to work off their energy. This practice of therapy by hibernation, this sleep-cure used on the people, may sometimes be successful; thus out of the conference around the green baize table comes the political selectiveness which enables Monsieur M'ba, the president of the Republic of Gabon, to state in all seriousness on his arrival in Paris for an official visit: "Gabon is independent, but between Gabon and France nothing has changed; everything goes on as before." In fact, the only change is that Monsieur M'ba is president of the Gabonese Republic and that he is received by the president of the French republic.

The colonialist bourgeoisie is helped in its work of calming down the natives by the inevitable religion. All those saints who have turned the other cheek, who have forgiven trespasses against them, and who have been spat on and insulted without shrinking are studied and held up as examples. On the other hand, the elite of the colonial countries, those slaves set free, when at the head of the movement inevitably end up by producing an ersatz conflict. They use their brothers' slavery to shame the slavedrivers or to provide an ideological policy of quaint humanitarianism for their oppressors' financial competitors. The truth is that they never make any real appeal to the aforesaid slaves; they never mobilize them in concrete terms. On the contrary, at the decisive moment (that is to say, from their point of view the moment of indecision) they brandish the danger of a "mass mobilization" as the crucial weapon which would bring about as if by magic the "end of the colonial regime." Obviously there are to be found at the core of the political parties and among their leaders certain revolutionaries who deliberately turn their backs upon the farce of national independence. But very quickly their questionings, their energy, and their anger obstruct the party machine; and these elements are gradually isolated, and then quite simply brushed aside. At this moment, as if there existed a dialectic concomitance, the colonialist police will fall upon them. With no security in the towns, avoided by the militants of their former party and rejected by its leaders, these undesirable firebrands will be stranded in county districts. Then it is that they will realize bewilderedly that the peasant masses catch on to what they have to say immediately, and without delay ask them the question to which they have not yet prepared the answer: "When do we start?". . .

A colonized people is not alone. In spite of all that colonialism can do, its frontiers remain open to new ideas and echoes from the world outside. It discovers that violence is in the atmosphere, that it here and there bursts out, and here and there sweeps away the colonial regime—that same violence which fulfills for the native a role that is not simply informatory, but also operative. The great victory of the Vietnamese people at Dien Bien Phu is no longer, strictly speaking, a Vietnamese victory. Since July, 1954, the question which the colonized peoples have asked themselves has been, "What must be done to bring about another Dien Bien Phu? How can we manage it?" Not a single colonized individual could ever again doubt the possibility of a Dien Bien Phu; the only problem was how best to use the forces at their disposal, how to organize them, and when to bring them into action. This encompassing violence does not work upon the colonized people only; it modifies the attitude of the colonialists who become aware of manifold Dien Bien Phus. This is why a veritable panic takes hold of the colonialist governments in turn. Their purpose is to capture the vanguard, to turn the movement of liberation toward the right, and to disarm the people: quick, quick, let's decolonize. . . .

But let us return to that atmosphere of violence, that violence which is just under the skin. We have seen that in its process toward maturity many leads are attached to it, to control it and show it the way out. Yet in spite of the metamorphoses which the colonial regime imposes upon it in the way of tribal or regional quarrels, that violence makes its way forward, and the native identifies his enemy and recognizes all his misfortunes, throwing all the exacerbated might of his hate and anger into this new channel. But how do we pass from the atmosphere of violence to violence in action? What makes the lid blow off? There is first of all the fact that this development does not leave the settler's blissful existence intact. The settler who "understands" the natives is made aware by several straws in the wind showing that something is afoot. "Good" natives become scarce; silence falls when the oppressor approaches; sometimes looks are black, and attitudes and remarks openly aggressive. The nationalist parties are astir, they hold a great many meetings, the police are increased and reinforce-ments of soldiers are brought in. The settlers, above all the farmers isolated on their land, are the first to become alarmed. They call for energetic measures.

The authorities do in fact take some spectacular measures. They arrest one or two leaders, they organize military parades and maneu-vers, and air force displays. But the demonstrations and warlike exercises, the smell of gunpowder which now fills the atmosphere, these things do not make the people draw back. Those bayonets and cannonades only serve to reinforce their aggressiveness. The atmos-phere becomes dramatic, and everyone wishes to show that he is ready for anything. And it is in these circumstances that the guns go off by themselves, for nerves are jangled, fear reigns and everyone is trigger-happy. A single commonplace incident is enough to start the machine-gunning. . . .

The repressions, far from calling a halt to the forward rush of na-tional consciousness, urge it on. Mass slaughter in the colonies at a certain stage of the embryonic development of consciousness increases that consciousness, for the hecatombs are an indication that between oppressors and oppressed everything can be solved by force. It must be remarked here that the political parties have not called for armed insurrection, and have made no preparations for such an insurrection. All these repressive measures, all those actions which are a result of fear are not within the leaders' intentions: they are overtaken by events. At this moment, then, colonialism may decide to arrest the nationalist leaders. But today the governments of colonized countries know very well that it is extremely dangerous to deprive the masses of their leaders; for then the people, unbridled, fling themselves into *jacqueries,* mutinies, and "brutish murders." The masses give free rein to their "bloodthirsty instincts" and force colonialism to free their leaders, to whom falls the difficult task of bringing them back to order. The colonized people, who have spontaneously brought their violence to the colossal task of destroying the colonial system, will very soon find themselves with the barren, inert slogan "Release X or Y." Then colonialism will release these men, and hold discussions with them. The time for dancing in the streets has come.

In certain circumstances, the party political machine may remain intact. But as a result of the colonialist repression and of the spontaneous reaction of the people the parties find themselves out-distanced by their militants. The violence of the masses is vigorously pitted against the military forces of the occupying power, and the situation deteriorates and comes to a head. Those leaders who are free remain, therefore, on the touchline. They have suddenly become useless, with their bureaucracy and their reasonable demands; yet we see them, far removed from events, attempting the crowning imposture—that of "speaking in the name of the silenced nation." As a general rule, colonialism welcomes this godsend with open arms, transforms these "blind mouths" into spokesmen, and in two minutes endows them with independence, on condition that they restore order.

So we see that all parties are aware of the power of such violence and that the question is not always to reply to it by a greater violence, but rather to see how to relax the tension.

What is the real nature of this violence? We have seen that it is the intuition of the colonized masses that their liberation must, and can only, be achieved by force. By what spiritual aberration do these men, without technique, starving and enfeebled, confronted with the military and economic might of the occupation, come to believe that violence alone will free them? How can they hope to triumph?

It is because violence (and this is the disgraceful thing) may constitute, in so far as it forms part of its system, the slogan of a political party. The leaders may call on the people to enter upon an armed struggle. This problematical question has to be thought over. When militarist Germany decides to settle its frontier disputes by force, we are not in the least surprised; but when the people of Angola, for example, decide to take up arms, when the Algerian people reject all means which are not violent, these are proofs that something has happened or is happening at this very moment. The colonized races, those slaves of modern times, are impatient. They know that this apparent folly alone can put them out of reach of colonial oppression. A new type of relations is established in the world. The underdeveloped peoples try to break their chains, and the extraordinary thing is that they succeed. . . .

. . . But it is a commonplace to observe and to say that in the majority of cases, for 95 per cent of the population of underdeveloped countries, independence brings no immediate change. The enlightened observer takes note of the existence of a kind of masked discontent, like the smoking ashes of a burnt-down house after the fire has been put out, which still threaten to burst into flames again.

So they say that the natives want to go too quickly. Now, let us never forget that only a very short time ago they complained of their slowness, their laziness, and their fatalism. Already we see that violence used in specific ways at the moment of the struggle for freedom does not magically disappear after the ceremony of trooping the national colors. It has all the less reason for disappearing since the reconstruction of the nation continues within the framework of cutthroat competition between capitalism and socialism.

This competition gives an almost universal dimension to even the most localized demands. Every meeting held, every act of repression committed, reverberates in the international arena. The murders of Sharpeville shook public opinion for months. In the newspapers, over the wavelengths, and in private conversations Sharpeville has become a symbol. It was through Sharpeville that men and women first became acquainted with the problem of apartheid in South Africa. Moreover, we cannot believe that demagogy alone is the explanation for the sudden interest the big powers show in the petty affairs of underdeveloped regions. Each *jacquerie,* each act of sedition in the Third World makes up part of a picture framed by the Cold War. Two men are beaten up in Salisbury, and at once the whole of a bloc goes into action, talks about those two men, and uses the beating-up incident to bring up the particular problem of Rhodesia, linking it, moreover, with the whole African question and with the whole question of colonized people. The other bloc however is equally concerned in measuring by the magnitude of the campaign the local weaknesses of its system. Thus the colonized peoples realize that neither clan remains outside local incidents. They no longer limit themselves to regional horizons, for they have caught on to the fact that they live in an atmosphere of international stress. . . .

. . . The atmosphere of violence, after having colored all the colonial phase, continues to dominate national life for . . . the Third World is not cut off from the rest. Quite the contrary, it is at the middle of the whirlpool. . . .

From *Studies in a Dying Colonialism* by Frantz Fanon, trans.
Haakon Chevalier (New York: Monthly Review Press, 1965), pp. 121–
26, 131–32. Reprinted by permission of the publisher.

Introduced into Algeria at the same time as racialism and humiliation, Western medical science, being part of the oppressive system,
has always provoked in the native an ambivalent attitude. This
ambivalence is in fact to be found in connection with all of the
occupier's modes of presence. With medicine we come to one of the
most tragic features of the colonial situation.

In all objectivity and in all humanity, it is a good thing that a
technically advanced country benefits from its knowledge and the
discoveries of its scientists. When the discipline considered concerns
man's health, when its very principle is to ease pain, it is clear that
no negative reaction can be justified. But the colonial situation is
precisely such that it drives the colonized to appraise all the colonizer's
contributions in a pejorative and absolute way. The colonized perceives
the doctor, the engineer, the schoolteacher, the policeman, the rural
constable, through the haze of an almost organic confusion. The
compulsory visit by the doctor to the *douar* is preceded by the assem-
bling of the population through the agency of the police authorities.
The doctor who arrives in this atmosphere of general constraint is
never a native doctor but always a doctor belonging to the dominant
society and very often to the army.

The statistics on sanitary improvements are not interpreted by the
native as progress in the fight against illness, in general, but as fresh
proof of the extension of the occupier's hold on the country. When
the French authorities show visitors through the Tizi-Ouzou sanitorium
or the operating units of the Mustapha hospital in Algiers, this has
for the native just one meaning: "This is what we have done for the
people of this country; this country owes us everything; were it not for
us, there would be no country." There is a real mental reservation on
the part of the native; it is difficult for him to be objective, to separate
the wheat from the chaff.

There are of course exceptions. In certain periods of calm, in
certain free confrontations, the colonized individual frankly recognizes
what is positive in the dominator's action. But this good faith is
immediately taken advantage of by the occupier and transformed
into a justification of the occupation. When the native, after a major
effort in the direction of truth, because he assumes that his defenses
have been surmounted, says, "That is good. I tell you so because I
think so," the colonizer perverts his meaning and translates, "Don't
leave, for what would we do without you?"

Thus, on the level of the whole colonized society, we always
discover this reluctance to qualify opposition to the colonialist, for
it so happens that every qualification is perceived by the occupier as

an invitation to perpetuate the oppression, as a confession of congenital impotence. The colonized people as a whole, when faced with certain happenings, will react in a harsh undifferentiated, categorical way before the dominant group's activity. It is not unusual to hear such extreme observations as this: "Nobody asked you for anything; who invited you to come? Take your hospitals and your port facilities and go home."

The fact is that the colonization, having been built on military conquest and the police system, sought a justification for its existence and the legitimization of its persistence in its works.

Reduced, in the name of truth and reason, to saying "yes" to certain innovations of the occupier, the colonized perceived that he thus became the prisoner of the entire system, and that the French medical service in Algeria could not be separated from French colonialism in Algeria. Then, as he could not cut himself off from his people, who aspired to a national existence on their own soil, he rejected doctors, schoolteachers, engineers, parachutists, all in one lump. . . .

At no time, in a non-colonial society, does the patient mistrust his doctor. On the level of technique, of knowledge, it is clear that a certain doubt can filter into the patient's mind, but this may be due to a hesitation on the part of the doctor which modifies the original confidence. This can happen anywhere. But it is obvious that certain circumstances can appreciably change the doctor-patient relationship. The German prisoner who was to be operated on by a French surgeon would very often, just before being given the anaesthetic, beseech the doctor not to kill him. Under the same circumstances, the surgeon might be more than ordinarily anxious to perform the operation successfully because of the other prisoners, because he realized the interpretation that might be given the event if a patient died on the operating table. The French prisoners in the German camps showed a similar concern when they asked the doctors working in the camp infirmary to assist in the operations performed by German surgeons. Literature and the motion pictures have made much of such situations, and after every war the problems they involve are commercially exploited.

In colonial territory such situations are to be found in even greater number. The sudden deaths of Algerians in hospitals, a common occurrence in any establishment caring for the sick and the injured, are interpreted as the effects of a murderous and deliberate decision, as the result of criminal maneuvers on the part of the European doctor. The Algerian's refusal to be hospitalized is always more or less related to that lingering doubt as to the colonial doctor's essential humanity. . . .

It is necessary to analyze, patiently and lucidly, each one of the reactions of the colonized, and every time we do not understand, we must tell ourselves that we are at the heart of the drama—that of the impossibility of finding a meeting ground in any colonial situation. For some time it was maintained that the native's reluctance to entrust himself to a European doctor was due to his attachment to his traditional medical techniques or to his dependence on the sorcerers or healers of his group. Such psychological reactions do obviously exist, and they were to be observed, not too many years ago, not only among the masses of generally advanced countries, but also among doctors themselves. . . . It is hardly abnormal . . . for individuals accustomed to practicing certain customs in the treatment of a given ailment, to adopting certain procedures when confronted with the disorder that illness constitutes, to refuse to abandon these customs and procedures because others are imposed on them, in other words because the new technique takes over completely and does not tolerate the persistence of any shred of tradition.

Here again we hear the same refrain:

If I abandon what I am in the habit of doing when my wife coughs and I authorize the European doctor to give her injections; if I find myself literally insulted and told I am a savage [this happens], because I have made scratches on the forehead of my son who has been complaining of a headache for three days; if I tell this insulter he is right and I admit that I was wrong to make those scratches which custom has taught me to do—if I do all these things I am acting, from a strictly rational point of view, in a positive way. For, as a matter of fact, my son has meningitis and it really has to be treated as a meningitis ought to be treated. But the colonial constellation is such that what should be the brotherly and tender insistence of one who wants only to help me is interpreted as a manifestation of the conqueror's arrogance and desire to humiliate.

It is not possible for the colonized society and the colonizing society to agree to pay tribute, at the same time and in the same place, to a single value. . . .

. . . [T]he colonial world reveals itself to be complex and extremely diverse in structure. There is always an opposition of exclusive worlds, a contradictory interaction of different techniques, a vehement confrontation of values.

The colonial situation does not only vitiate the relations between doctor and patient. We have shown that the doctor always appears as a link in the colonialist network, as a spokesman for the occupying power. We shall see that this ambivalence of the patient before medical technique is to be found even when the doctor belongs to the dominated people. There is a manifest ambivalence of the colonized group with respect to any member who acquires a technique or the manners of the conqueror. For the group, in fact, the native technician is living proof that any one of its members is capable of being an engineer, a lawyer or a doctor. But there is at the same time, in the background, the awareness of a sudden divergence between the homogeneous group, enclosed within itself, and this native technician who has escaped beyond the specific psychological or emotional categories of the people. The native doctor is a Europeanized, Westernized doctor, and in certain circumstances he is considered as no longer being a part of the dominated society. He is tacitly rejected into the camp of the oppressors, into the opposing camp. It is not by accident that in certain colonies the educated native is referred to as "having acquired the habits of a master."

For many of the colonized, the native doctor is compared to the native police, to the *caïd*, to the notable. The colonized is both proud of the success of his *race* and at the same time looks upon this technician with disapproval. The native doctor's behavior with respect to the traditional medicine of his country is for a long time characterized by a considerable aggressiveness.

The native doctor feels himself psychologically compelled to demonstrate firmly his new admission to a rational universe. This accounts for the abrupt way in which he rejects the magic practices of his people. Given the ambivalence of the colonized with respect to the native doctor and the ambivalence of the native doctor before certain features of his culture, the encounter of doctor and patient inevitably proves difficult. The colonized patient is the first to set the tone. Once the superiority of Western technique over traditional methods of treatment is recognized, it is thought preferable to turn to the colonizers who are, after all, "the true possessors of the technique." . . . The native doctor, because of the operation of the complex psychological laws that govern colonial society, frequently finds himself in a difficult position.

A View from 1878

In 1878 William Ewart Gladstone, writing for the British magazine *The Nineteenth Century*, summarized the nature of "the sentiment of empire." As Britain's great Liberal prime minister of the Victorian age, he spoke for a wide spectrum of anti-imperial opinion. At the time he wrote the words below, Benjamin Disraeli, Gladstone's opponent, was Prime Minister.

From "England's Mission" by William Ewart Gladstone, *The Nineteenth Century*, IV (September, 1878), 569–70.

The sentiment of empire may be called innate in every Briton. If there are exceptions, they are like those of men born blind or lame among us. It is part of our patrimony: born with our birth, dying only with our death; incorporating itself in the first elements of our knowledge, and interwoven with all our habits of mental action upon public affairs. It is a portion of our national stock, which has never been deficient, but which has more than once run to rank excess, and brought us to mischief accordingly, mischief that for a time we have weakly thought was ruin. In its normal action, it made for us the American colonies, the grandest monument ever erected by a people of modern times, and second only to the Greek colonisation in the whole history of the world. In its domineering excess, always under the name of British interests and British honour, it lost them by obstinacy and pride. Lord Chatham who forbade us to tax, Mr. [Edmund] Burke who forbade us to legislate for them, would have saved them. But they had to argue for a limitation of English power; and to meet the reproach of the political wiseacres, who first blustered on our greatness, and then, when they reaped as they had sown, whined over our calamities. Undoubtedly the peace of 1782–3, with its adjuncts in exasperated feeling, was a terrible dismemberment. But England was England still: and one of the damning signs of the politics of the school is their total blindness to the fact, that the central strength of England lies in England. Their eye travels with satisfaction over the wide space upon the map covered by the huge ice-bound deserts of North America or the unpenetrated wastes of Australasia, but rests with mortification on the narrow bounds of latitude and longitude marked by nature for the United Kingdom. They are the materialists of politics: their faith is in acres and in leagues, in sounding titles and long lists of territories. They forget that the entire fabric of the British Empire was reared and consolidated by the energies of a people, which was (though it is not now) insignificant in numbers, when compared with the leading States of the Continent; and that if by some vast convulsion our transmarine possessions could be all submerged, the very same energies of that very same people would either discover other inhabited or inhabitable spaces of the globe on which to repeat its work, or would without them in other modes assert its undiminished greatness. Of all the opinions disparaging to England, there is not one which can lower her like that which teaches that the source of strength for this almost measureless body lies in its extremities, and not in the heart which has so long propelled the blood through all its regions, and in the brain which has bound and binds them into one.

In the sphere of personal life, most men are misled through the medium of the dominant faculty of their nature. It is round that dominant faculty that folly and flattery are wont to buzz. They play upon vainglory by exaggerating and commending what it does, and by piquing it on what it sees cause to forbear from doing. It is so with nations. For all of them the supreme want really is, to be warned against the indulgence of the dominant passion. The dominant passion of France was military glory. Twice, in this century, it has towered beyond what is allowed to man; and twice has paid the tremendous forfeit of opening to the foe the proudest capital in the world. The dominant passion of England is extended empire. It has heretofore been kept in check by the integrity and sagacity of her statesmen, who have not shrunk from teaching her the lessons of self-denial and self-restraint. But a new race has arisen; and the most essential or the noblest among all the duties of government, the exercise of moral control over ambition and cupidity, have been left to the intermittent and feeble handling of those who do not govern.

Between the two parties in this controversy there is a perfect agreement that England has a mighty mission in the world; but there is a discord as fundamental upon the question what that mission is.

A View from the 1960s

Kenneth Robinson, a British administrator and scholar who had known the colonial service at first hand, but who also had been able to step away from it into the groves of academe, was invited in 1963 to speak on the problem of "trusteeship" at Acadia University in Nova Scotia. He used the occasion to present an incisive, if yet interim, statement about the nature of those dilemmas which plagued the imperial administrators in the field and at home, as well as the latter-day scholars who sought to understand them and the phenomenon they fed—imperialism. Robinson was then Director of the Institute of Commonwealth Studies in London; he is now Vice-Chancellor of the University of Hong Kong. In the third of his series of talks, he provided the evaluation of imperialism that concludes our selections.

From *The Dilemmas of Trusteeship: Aspects of British Colonial Policy Between the Wars* by Kenneth Robinson (London: Oxford University Press, 1965), pp. 65–94. Reprinted by permission of the author and the publisher.

The government of dependencies "whose population" was not "in a sufficiently advanced state to be fitted for representative government" and which "if held at all, must be governed by the dominant country, or by persons delegated for that purpose by it" was, Mill asserted, "as legitimate as any other, if it is the one which in the existing state of civilization of the subject people, most facilitates their transition to a higher stage of improvement." For such government the ideal form was that of an enlightened bureaucratic despotism. "We need not expect," Mill continued, "to see that ideal realized; but unless some approach to it is, the rulers are guilty of a dereliction of the highest moral trust which can devolve upon a nation: and if they do not even aim at it, they are selfish usurpers." In this Mill echoed Burke: "all political power which is set over men . . . ought to be *some way or other* exercised for their benefit." The realistic moderation with which these great men expressed the idea of trusteeship has been less remarked than the idea itself.

Nor were their arguments directed to justifying the seizure of power in territories hitherto free. It was the expansion of European, and the emergence of American, imperialism at the end of the nineteenth century which focused attention once again on that more intractable issue, an era when, even in the jungle of sovereign states, naked force was still felt to need some justification.

It is difficult for the strongest advocate of national rights to assert that the people in actual occupation or political control over a given area of the earth are entitled to do what they will with "their own," entirely disregarding the direct and indirect consequences of their actions upon the rest of the world. . . . There is nothing unworthy, quite the contrary, in the notion that nations which, through a more stimulative environment, have advanced further in certain arts of industry, politics, or morals, should communicate these to nations which from their circumstances were more backward, so as to aid them in developing alike the material resources of their land and the spiritual qualities of their people. Nor is it clear that in this work some . . "compulsion" is wholly illegitimate. Force is itself no remedy, coercion is not education, but it may be a prior condition to the operation of educative forces . . . it follows that civilized Governments *may* undertake the political and economic control of lower races . . . What, then, are the conditions which render it legitimate? They may be provisionally stated thus: Such interference . . . must be directed primarily to secure the safety and progress of the civilization of the world, and not the special interest of the interfering nation. Such interference must be attended by an improvement and elevation of the character of the people who are brought under this control. Lastly, the determination of the two preceding conditions must not be left to the arbitrary will or judgment of the interfering nation, but must proceed from some organized representation of civilized humanity.

J. A. Hobson, from whose famous . . . book *Imperialism* I have been quoting, did not, you will notice, contend that to be legitimate Imperial rule must benefit the "lower races" alone or even that the advantages they secured from it must be the maximum possible but merely that their condition must be improved. But he added another condition which, on the face of it, has nothing to do with their advantage. This too is stated with studied moderation. Imperial rule is also to be directed "primarily to secure the safety and the progress of . . . the world, and not the special interest of" the imperial power. It is not argued that this condition is necessary for the benefit of the subject people but as a rule for international policy. Hobson certainly did not "expect to see" these ideals realized, or even approached. "The true conditions for the exercise of such a 'trust'" were, he wrote, "entirely lacking." His opinion was, of course, that the contemporary development of the advanced capitalist countries at the beginning of this century was such as entirely to preclude the possibility of colonial trusteeship.

Twenty years later Lugard restated in the *Dual Mandate* what had long been the official defence of British Imperialism.

The tropics are the heritage of mankind, and neither, on the one hand, has the suzerain Power a right to their exclusive exploitation, nor, on the other hand, have the races which inhabit them a right to deny their bounties to those who need them. . . . The policy of the "open door," has two distinct though mutually dependent aspects— viz., equal opportunity to the commerce of other countries, and an unrestricted market to the native producer. The tropics can only be successfully developed if the interests of the controlling Power are identical with those of the natives of the country, and it seeks no individual advantage, and imposes no restriction for its own benefit.

Like other Imperialists, Lugard believed passionately in his ideal and saw no reason why it should not, by and large, be realized. But the proclamation of the Dual Mandate received its classical expression, like many another doctrine of social and economic policy, just when the conditions which had made it seem plausible were beginning to disappear. Was the doctrine of trusteeship necessarily dependent on the conception of a self-regulating harmonization of interests which the classical theory of free competition assumed? It was one thing to claim that the Open Door was, as Hobson had implied, the necessary condition of international acquiescence in the powers that imperial states claimed for themselves over large areas of the world. It was surely quite another to claim that it was a sufficient condition that native interests would not be exploited. Open competition by traders of all nations would, the argument went, assure the colonial producers fair prices for their exports and equally assure colonial consumers fair prices for their imports. But what if colonial conditions were such that competition was more than usually imperfect? . . .

Was it not unlikely that, taking the sphere of colonial government as a whole, the interests of the colonial power should be *identical* with those of the natives? Trusteeship suffered greatly from the overstatement of self-justification. The aggregates with which it worked were sums which could not, in fact, be added up. Even in the strictly economic sphere, the techniques which might make it possible to calculate the share of national product that accrued to natives and non-natives, to residents in a colony and non-residents, had not yet been invented and, if they had been, sketchy colonial administrations had hardly begun, even at the end of the second [world] war, to produce the data needed for such calculations.

How, again, could a balance be struck between the social changes that any economic development must bring and native satisfactions within their own social order? The ideas of Lugard and his followers brought this problem into much greater prominence just at a time when the easy assumption of the obvious superiority of Western civilization was sharply shaken by the first [world] war, and the increasingly evident incapacity of the Western economic system to solve the problem of unemployment. They were soon reinforced by the much greater knowledge which anthropologists and administrators began to make available of the complex purposes which native social organization served. A large new area of uncertainty was thus added to the problem.

Let me illustrate this. Hobson had considered that "the true 'imperial' policy" was "best illustrated" by Basutoland [1] which had been rescued from the industrial exploiters, where the old political and economic institutions were preserved, the British authorities interfering as little as possible with native ways. Europeans were not allowed to hold land or to prospect for minerals and needed a licence even to open a store. In 1935 a Commissioner sent out by the British government reported—I quote [historian] Sir Keith Hancock's summary of his findings—that

> Economically there was a great deal to hope for from the agricultural and pastoral resources of the country and the intelligence of its people. But the resources had been squandered, and the intelligence left without guidance. The administration had done nothing effective to check erosion, which was occurring on a scale that threatened "the whole fabric of the soil." It had nothing to check stock theft, which was occurring on a scale that threatened to undermine both the moral integrity and the economic productivity of the Basuto people. It had not even been effective in collecting the taxes that were its due. Basutoland suffered from a lack of governance which was sometimes dignified with the title of "indirect rule." Never since the British government first took to itself responsibility for Basutoland, Sir Alan Pim[2] said, had it given the country rule of any sort, direct or indirect. Indirect rule meant the incorporation of Native institutions into a single system of government, under the "continuous guidance, supervision, and stimulus of European officers." It regarded Native institutions, not as an end, but as a means towards the development and welfare of the Native people to whom the institutions belonged. But in Basutoland the Chiefs of the family of Moshesh had been allowed to go their own irresponsible and increasingly prodigal way; there were two parallel sets of institutions in the country, and both of them were futile.

Sir Alan Pim also reported that more than 50 per cent of the adult male Basutos were at any one time normally absent, working on the farms and mines of the Union of South Africa, a figure, he pointed out, "in striking contrast to the estimate made by the Belgian Congo Committee of 1924–5" in whose opinion "not more than five per cent. could be absent for long periods, and an additional five per cent. within two days' journey, without definitely harmful effects to tribal life. Part of the remedy he proposed was that Basutoland should adopt the Nigerian system of native administration with its closer European

[1] [Now Lesotho.]
[2] [Author of a 1935 report on the Basuto and the drought of 1932–33.]

control of native institutions and attempt to adapt them to the new needs of economic and social development as opposed to the almost complete absence of "interference" with native society which Hobson had esteemed the ideal.

But in the home of the native administration system, in Nigeria itself, in areas where export crops were produced by African small-holders, a new problem was already posing the question of what was to be done to adapt Native Authorities to the needs of a society in which, as in Western Nigeria, economic growth had already by the mid-thirties produced in fair number new classes unknown to tra-ditional society, cocoa brokers, traders, lorry and bus operators, farm-ers employing labour, school teachers, and was resulting in growing urban areas in which the coexistence of many different ethnic groups made the maintenance or extension of traditional native authority doubtfully effective. How far, in short, even in the most favourable circumstances, where large-scale European plantations or mines, let alone European settlement, did not exist, was it possible or desirable to try to maintain or adapt the native social system? What, in such circumstances, were "native" interests and how, even if they could be ascertained, could they be reconciled with "European" interests in the maintenance of law and order and the provision of social services especially those all-important but unpopular public health measures so vital to continued European activity as well as to the natives them-selves. Nor, of course, was this a specifically African problem: it was indeed more sharply posed in Malaya where so many of the new forces were expressed in the activities of Chinese and Indian im-migrants, the legacy of an earlier age which could not simply be ex-punged, and where the attempt to maintain the authority of the Sultans ran up against the paramount pressure for a greater degree of administrative unity which the development of the economy increas-ingly demanded.

But if, even as formulated in the more extended version of the Dual Mandate, the principle of trusteeship thus did not provide any un-ambiguous answer to the actual problems of colonial government either in the economic or the wider social sphere, neither did it pro-vide very specific guidance in the sphere of politics. It emphasized . . . that the ultimate responsibility for the general governance of the affairs of the Colonial Empire must . . . rest with the British govern-ment. This followed, conveniently enough, from the Dual Mandate itself: the responsibilities which the trustee had felt justified in as-suming in the joint interests of the world and the colonial peoples evidently could not, on that basis, be laid aside, until the ward could reasonably be regarded as equipped to discharge them himself. But moreover, certain further deductions could be drawn. . . . Fitness for self-government might be held to imply, first the ability to give modern trade and industry the security they need, second the ability to afford security of person and good government by the standards of western Europe, and third the ability to produce native rulers strong enough and responsible enough to respect international law. . . . On the doctrine that the British were trustees for world interests, it could be inferred that their responsibilities could properly be handed over only if a native government had been brought into existence capable of satisfying at least the first condition, probably also the third, but conceivably the second as well.

A quite different criterion of that fitness for self-government which would justify the trustee in handing over to the ward could, however, be deduced from the second half of the Dual Mandate, the doctrine that the British were also trustees for the welfare of the native races. This might be defined as "the ability to work the institutions that make democracy and freedom effective." The Labour Party was using this line of argument when—no doubt with the Kenya settlers' claims in mind—it said in its 1928 policy statement that "imperial responsibility . . . will be maintained during the period preceding the establishment of democratic institutions." But though it was possible, it was evidently not necessary to take the view that democracy was the only form of government to which a proper regard for the welfare of the colonial peoples would allow the trustee to relinquish his responsibilities. In the political sphere, as in the economic and social spheres, the principle of trusteeship thus provided no unambiguous answer, still less did it help to prescribe the all-important intermediate steps.

Such light as, even in its Dual Mandate model, the torch of trusteeship could be made to yield thus seemed to illumine far more clearly one or two paths *not* to be followed rather than any definite road forward through the still largely unknown, extraordinarily varied and usually deceptive country which the application of Western technology, in however modest a form, the growth of the market, and research in the natural and social sciences, were just beginning to disclose in the Colonial Empire. The more thoroughgoing advocates of the principle of trusteeship would never have allowed that it is only in a revolutionary phase, and then rather briefly, that general principles are at all seen as susceptible of complete and direct application in politics. In a well-established order, on the other hand, politics are understood, though not always admitted, to call, in a necessarily imperfect world, for "the endless composition of claims in conflict." . . .

Again, if brought to bear at all, the principle of trusteeship, like any other, had to be brought to bear in each territory on an historically determined situation, in which the actions of the past, however reprehensible the principles then at work, had created responsibilities which could not simply be liquidated. Many a harassed Colonial Secretary might have agreed that it would have been more convenient, as well as possibly more virtuous, if Indian or Chinese labour had never been brought to territories like Malaya, Fiji, Trinidad, or British Guiana, or if European settlement had not been officially encouraged in Kenya in 1903 or in Palestine after the first world war, or if Britain had not in Ceylon or Cyprus found herself in control of territories where, in a far more remote past, earlier colonizations had produced sizeable minorities, like the Ceylon Tamils or the Cypriot Turks, wholly distinct in language and culture from the majority of people. But, confronted with such situations, had not the imperial power responsibilities, not merely to the majority, or to those who could claim to be the indigenous people, but to *all* the inhabitants? This line of thought, as natural to the rulers of an old-established multi-national state as it has seemed to their critics inevitable in an Imperialist policy of "divide and rule," appears again and again in their pronouncements of policy. It was the basis of the restatement of trusteeship implicit in the Report of the Joint Select Committee on Closer Union in East Africa. The famous declaration of 1923 that in Kenya "the interests of the African natives must be paramount, and if and when those interests and the interests of the immigrant races should conflict, the former should prevail," meant, said the Joint Select Committee, "no more than that the interests of the overwhelming majority of the indigenous population should not be subordinated to those of a minority belonging to another race, however important in itself." Similarly, in 1938, Malcolm MacDonald, then Colonial Secretary, rejected an opposition motion that the primary purpose of colonial policy should be the welfare and progress of the native inhabitants, claiming that it was, on the contrary, the welfare and progress of *all* the inhabitants, though, he went on, "our first duty" was "always" to the native inhabitants.

If the principle of trusteeship was thus reduced to the exceedingly modest aim that imperial power must be, in Burke's words, *"some way or other* exercised for the benefit" of the colonial peoples, it has also to be recognized that, such as it was, it could in any event operate only within the fairly narrow, if fluctuating, limits defined by the strategic preoccupations of British statesmen, the economic pressures to which they responded, and the reluctance to surrender power from which they were by no means exempt, even if temperament and experience combined to give them a flexibility not often displayed by imperial rulers. Egypt, though it was never a colony and its independence had been unilaterally declared by Britain in 1922, most strikingly displays the distortion of trusteeship by defence, but Malta, Gibraltar, and Cyprus all illustrated how changing conceptions of strategic needs set limits for colonial policy makers.

It is essential to underline the limits which were set to any simple application of trusteeship by the facts of history, the imperatives of defence, and the more insidious pressures of British economic interest. It is only common sense to admit not only the ambiguities inherent in the idea of trusteeship itself, but also the uncertainties imposed by the likelihood of mistakes in estimating the consequences of policy which was certainly greater in the Colonial Empire than in more developed countries. But it is also necessary to allow that there was an area of decision in colonial policy in which the demands of trusteeship, if by no means always conceded, yet significantly affected the outcome. The greatest disservice which the too complacent reiteration of the professions of trusteeship has done to a true estimation of the late phase of British imperial rule is to have strengthened the counter myth which denies it any place at all. . . .

. . . [T]he most perplexing problem of colonial policy in the interwar years was one in which not even the rough and ready calculus of economic aggregates, had it then been available, would have served to test the aims of policy. It was, paradoxically, the one in which the experts, both academic and official, tended to be most certain of the fundamental rightness of the dominant ideas. Yet it was also one in which no policy could rest, in the last analysis, on more than judgements of value made by the policy makers themselves. Was the task of trusteeship, so far as those narrow limits of history, power, and economic pressure might allow, one of transforming colonial society into a modern western civilization, however long that might take? Or was it to preserve, so far as might be, the traditional order of native society, purged of its grosser abuses, in Western eyes (cannibalism, for example) so that it might be enabled to survive until the native peoples were "able to stand by themselves"? "Indirect Rule"— it is time to give this school of thought the name by which, rather misleadingly, it was generally known—did not argue that the traditional institutions of native society should be preserved unchanged (as Hobson had gone far to imply) or that they could be left entirely free to make their own adaptation to the new demands which were bound to follow the imposition of colonial rule. The task was to assist them to make that adaptation. Changes so great that such an adaptation evidently could not be made must therefore not be introduced. Economic development and education should accordingly be promoted only so far as seemed likely to prove consistent with that over-riding purpose. It was for instance because the native social institutions whose disintegration they wished to prevent had developed in intimate relationship with an agricultural environment that advocates of indirect rule from Lugard onwards so strongly urged that native peasant production should be the basis of economic development. "Indirect rule" called for a gradual blending of modern Western and traditional native elements without attempting to prescribe in advance what character the mixture should ultimately attain. . . .

Indirect rule had three major weaknesses. It demanded of the European agents of control an alert empiricism informed not only by conviction of the value to any people of its own social values and institutions but also by a detailed knowledge of those institutions and of the precise impact on them of the varied social and economic results of Western rule. Such knowledge, even in most favourable circumstances, they could never attain. Secondly, native social institutions, especially in Africa, varied greatly in the extent to which they could effectively be utilized even for the simplest purposes of administration, let alone as the chosen instruments of that social reintegration which the inroads of modernity were making desperately urgent in some areas while others even in the same territory seemed to have remained largely untouched by their impact. Changes which could readily be absorbed, for example by the great Moslem emirates of Northern Nigeria with their well-developed systems of local administration and taxation, could not possibly be accommodated by communities of a few thousand people with no central authority more elaborate than a gathering of family heads. Thirdly, even the largest and most highly organized native states were an uncertain basis on which to construct any institutions which looked like being able to support the management of the central services of the territories of which they now formed only a relatively small part. It was these two factors, the immense range of native societies which colonial rule brought within a single administrative unit and the territorial unevenness of the social change it induced, that proved incompatible with the ideas of indirect rule.

Local administration apart, it was in educational policy that those ideas had their greatest influence, assisted by a widespread anxiety to avoid reproducing what were considered the dangerous results of educational policy in India. Insistence on the use of native languages in the earlier years of schooling, attempts to give education a more practical bent, and a desire to see more attention given at the secondary stage to vocational rather than literary or general education all reflected this approach. But, especially in Africa, other influences, of which shortage of money was not the least important, resulted in a policy of close co-operation in education with the missions, which provided almost all primary, as well as many secondary, schools and teacher training besides. Although their leading authorities accepted a good deal of this general approach to educational policy, there was a great variety in its actual application. Without the missions, practice might well have been more influenced by hostility to "literary" education and by some of the more doctrinaire enthusiasts for its adaptation, not to the developing needs of Africa, but to features of traditional society destined to diminishing importance. But in their fundamental approach, the educational policy makers were surely thinking on the right lines, even if that approach was distorted by some of the more conservative administrators and also by Africans determined not to be fobbed off with what they deemed a second best in education. The new independent states of Africa and Asia, which are certainly not going to be replicas of any Western country, are rediscovering the vital importance of reshaping education to meet the actual needs of native society.

To turn, finally, to the political implications of trusteeship. . . . British policy never, in the inter-war years or earlier, contemplated the eventual incorporation of the colonial territories in a Greater Britain. There was a general impression, it can hardly be called more than that, that local participation in colonial government was desirable and could be progressively increased as capacity for such participation developed, which often meant as the pressure for it became too great to be conveniently resisted. If British policy was certainly not opposed in principle to any idea of eventual self-government it equally certainly did not during the inter-war years conceive it to be part of its duty "officiously to strive" to bring self-government into existence. A substantial proportion of that relatively small group who were closely and actively concerned with colonial policy was wholly sceptical of any idea that, in the Colonial Empire, self-government was likely to be achieved by the development of parliamentary, still less democratic, institutions. To the people who had, after all, invented parliamentary government, the extent of political consensus that it requires for its continued existence was quite well understood. But with that understanding went a profound conviction that political development was not to be brought about by social engineering, by elaborate constitutional provisions supported by social planning. Rather, it must be an organic growth, fostered by habits of accommodation, which were taken to be the supreme art in politics. There resulted an assumption that piecemeal concessions of varying degrees of participation in government might be expected somehow to result in the development of political habits which could in the long run be translated into an institutional basis for self-government appropriate to the varying genius of the inhabitants of a given territory.

For all the scepticism of the professionals, British opinion, especially liberal opinion, continually underestimated the strength of feeling that representative institutions, however remote they might be from achieving responsible government, invariably aroused in communally divided countries. For all their experience in Ireland and India, they remained hopeful that experience would teach the habit of accommodation. Here too, history had imposed a limitation which the

British never quite brought themselves to think of trying to remove. In virtually every territory a Legislative Council has been established at a time when the unofficials to be appointed to it were mostly members of the local British business and professional community. It might still have an official majority—almost all of them had during the inter-war years—but it had the functions and many of the ceremonial procedures of a parliament, and it was inevitable that, as a native educated and professional class emerged, its members too should seek representation in that legislature and look to its eventual development as a genuine local parliament. Convinced of the entire incompatibility of such a development with their ideals, the "indirect rule" administrators concentrated on limiting the territorial scope of the Councils wherever possible and so missed the opportunity of reconciling the native authority system with the need for territorial political unity which might have been provided by arranging for Legislative Councils made up of representatives of the Native authorities. Far sighted in this as in most other things, [Sir Gordon] Guggisberg arranged such a link in the Gold Coast Colony in 1925 but the only other territory in which anything similar was done was Fiji where it long survived as the basis of Fijian representation.

So long as Legislative Councils existed they were bound to suggest development by well-recognized stages—elected minority, unofficial majority, elected majority, responsible government. The combined effect of this fact and the habit of mind I have tried to describe was the gradual development in the inter-war years of the theory that while British overall responsibility would continue for an indefinite period, colonial governments would pass through progressive stages to eventual self-government. And although this did not necessarily imply parliamentary government, no alternative was suggested. . . .

The British habit of setting up each territory as a separate unit of administration and government, with its own budget, laws and public services, has unquestionably been a powerful factor in fostering colonial nationalism and also, where the unit was a suitable one to serve as the basis of a state, self-government of some kind. But another aspect of this habitual approach was a tendency to accept whatever units the British found themselves confronted with and to maintain them—even within a larger territory which for other purposes they administered as a single entity—without considering what effect maintaining such smaller units must necessarily have on the possible emergence of any unit suitable to provide the basis for a state of any kind. It was, for instance, initially convenient in Malaya nominally to govern through the Sultans and in consequence nine separate Malay States were retained in this small area. The indirect rule system in Africa provides many similar examples in Uganda, Nigeria, and

Ghana. Moreover, this tendency applied not only to territorial units, but to racial communities or minorities, which were themselves often treated as separate units for many purposes of government, as, for example, the Chinese Protectorate in the Straits Settlements whereby a special set of officials administered the Chinese through their own community leaders, or the Fijian administration in Fiji under which the affairs of Fijians were in almost all important matters in the hands of a separate organization of government, which resembled a state within a state. Arrangements of this kind may be the basis, for the community concerned, of some degree of self-government within a colonial system but they are not likely to promote any national self-government within the territory as a whole or the gradual development of a habit of accommodation between different communities which the idea of organic political growth demands. In saying this, I am not suggesting either that regional or communal loyalties in such territories are fictitious or that it is at all easy for a colonial ruler to reduce their force, but only that arrangements of this kind can hardly be regarded as exemplifying stages in any development towards self-government on a national basis in each territory, such as the progressive theory implied.

The problems of trusteeship were the problems of power, of the responsibilities of the strong towards the weak. The unequal distribution of political and economic power in the world, which was the fundamental basis of colonialism, has not been suddenly abolished by the accession of most colonies to political independence. The idea of trusteeship could not, any more than any other general principle, supply a clear and definite prescription of the proper role of a colonial power in the enormous variety of actual situations which confronted British rulers in the Colonial Empire. But whenever a serious and sustained attempt was made to bring it to bear on the actual circumstances of a particular territory it brought into much sharper relief specific problems inherent in such a relationship. With the end of the colonial era, it is for the rulers of the new independent states to judge what their responsibilities for the welfare of their own people require. But the rich and powerful countries of the world are not thereby absolved from any further responsibility towards those countries. Now, as earlier, their interest as well as their duty should impel them to seek to reduce the international tensions that result from these great disparities in wealth and power. In that stupendous task, the search for reciprocities of interest, which was at the heart of the trusteeship idea, remains more likely to provide a viable basis for the relationship between a rich and strong and a poor and weak country than the unmitigated national altruism, or national egotism which are too often proffered to us today as the only moral or rational bases of policy. Greatly changed though their terms have been by the disappearance of western European colonial rule, the dilemmas of trusteeship remain, as the young [Winston] Churchill wrote of East Africa more than half a century ago, "the problems of the world."

For Further Reading

The literature on imperialism is vast, as is that on each of the societies over which the European powers exercised control. Much of that literature is reviewed, for the British Empire, in Robin W. Winks, ed., *The Historiography of the British Empire-Commonwealth* (Durham, N.C., 1966). The literature on the Dutch is summarized in W. Ph. Coolhaas, *A Critical Survey of Studies on Dutch Colonial History* (The Hague, 1960) and that on the Germans in Prosser Gifford and Wm. Roger Louis, eds., *Britain and Germany in Africa: Imperial Rivalry and Colonial Rule* (New Haven, 1967). There is no comparable assessment in English of the French literature.

A succinct and readable survey is Raymond F. Betts, *Europe Overseas: Phases of Imperialism* (New York, 1968). Longer, and more consistently comparative in its approach, is David K. Fieldhouse, *The Colonial Empires from the Eighteenth Century* (New York, 1966). Parker T. Moon, *Imperialism and World Politics* (New York, 1926), continues to be the best survey of the interrelations between imperial rivalry and World War I. A. P. Thornton, *Doctrines of Imperialism* (New York, 1965) and his *The Imperial Idea and Its Enemies* (London, 1963) provide a sophisticated and theoretical treatment of the justifications for, and attacks upon, imperialism. Robert A. Huttenback, *The British Imperial Experience* (New York, 1966), Henri Brunschwig, *French Colonialism, 1871–1914: Myths and Realities* (London, 1966), and Raymond F. Betts, *Assimilation and Association in French Colonial Theory, 1890–1914* (New York, 1961) provide lively and brief coverage of their subjects.

Who were the imperialists? One must still turn to biography for the answer. Richard Faber, *The Vision and the Need: Late Victorian Imperialist Aims* (London, 1966) reveals the views of ten from Britain. C. A. Bodelsen, *Studies in Mid-Victorian Imperialism* (Copenhagen, 1924) examines a somewhat different group. Robert Heussler, *Yesterday's Rulers: The Making of the British Colonial Service* (Syracuse, 1963) explores methods of recruitment. Stephen H. Roberts, *The History of French Colonial Policy, 1870–1925* (London, 1929) does not ignore the role of the individual. A generally poor book not entirely without merits, W. O. Henderson's *Studies in German Colonial History* (London, 1962), brings together a series of essays. Margery Perham, *Lugard*, in particular *The Years of Adventure, 1858–1898* (London, 1956), is excellent and revealing reading, while Philip

Magnus, *Kitchener: Portrait of an Imperialist* (London, 1958) recounts the exploits of a proconsul. Roland Oliver, *Sir Harry Johnston and the Scramble for Africa* (London, 1957) and R. E. Wraith, *Guggisberg* (London, 1967) are good biographies of major figures. Guggisberg was Governor of the Gold Coast, which was to become Ghana, from 1919 to 1927.

The Europeans' conception of the strange new worlds to which they went varied between wonder, bafflement, frustration, and indifference. The permutations of these moods may be examined in five generally excellent books, all largely but not exclusively British in their orientation: Philip D. Curtin, *The Image of Africa* (Madison, Wisc., 1964), Bernard Smith, *European Vision and the South Pacific, 1768–1850* (Oxford, 1960), Helen G. Trager, *Burma through Alien Eyes* (New York [1966]), George D. Bearce, *British Attitudes toward India, 1784–1858* (Oxford, 1961), and Eric Stokes, *The English Utilitarians and India* (Oxford, 1959). For a later period and a different empire, Wolfe W. Schmokel, *Dream of Empire: German Colonialism, 1919–1945* (New Haven, 1964) is sound.

Literature on indigenous reactions to the European presence is slight but growing. This is especially true for India and is becoming true for Africa; several relevant titles are cited in the pertinent essays in Winks, ed., *Historiography,* mentioned above. Two books by Frantz Fanon, *The Wretched of the Earth* (New York, 1968—originally published in Paris in 1961 as *Les damnés de la terre*) and *A Dying Colonialism* (New York, 1967—originally published in Paris in 1959 as *L' An Cinq de la révolution Algérienne*) are essential reading, as is O. Mannoni, *Prospero and Caliban: The Psychology of Colonization,* 2nd ed. (New York, 1964—originally published in Paris in 1950 as *Psychologie de la colonisation*). Against these might be set two superior collections of occasional pieces, A. P. Thornton, *For the File on Empire* (London, 1968) and Margery Perham, *Colonial Sequence, 1930 to 1949* (London, 1967). One should also read William R. Roff, *The Origins of Malay Nationalism* (New Haven, 1967).

Other titles are listed in Stewart C. Easton, *The Rise and Fall of Western Colonialism* (New York, 1964), George H. Nadel and Perry Curtis, eds., *Imperialism and Colonialism* (New York, 1964), Robin W. Winks, ed., *British Imperialism* (New York, 1963), and Harrison M. Wright, ed., *The "New Imperialism": Analysis of Late Nineteenth-Century Expansion* (Boston, 1961). The last is the best.